Working with the Self-Absorbed

How to Handle Narcissistic Personalities on the Job

Nina Brown, Ed.D., LPC, NCC

New Harbinger Publications, Inc.

Distributed in Canada by Raincoast Books

Copyright © 2002 by Nina Brown
           New Harbinger Publications, Inc.
           5674 Shattuck Avenue
           Oakland, CA 94609

Cover design by Blue Designs
Edited by Carol Honeychurch
Text design by Tracy Powell-Carlson

ISBN-10 1-57224-292-2
ISBN-13 978-1-57224-292-0

New Harbinger Publications' website address: www.newharbinger.com

09   08   07

10   9   8   7   6   5   4   3   2

This book is dedicated to my grandchildren, Billy, Joey, Samantha, Christopher, Nicholas, and Emma. I hope that they never have to work with or for a destructive narcissist.

Contents

Acknowledgments

No book can be writeen and published without encouragement and support, and this one in no exception. I received encouragement (although some would call it nagging) from two colleagues, Bill Drewry and Jim Cross. I learned much about destructive and pathological narcissism from clinical experiences of my colleagues at the Mid-Atlantic Group Psychotherapy Society and the American Froup Psychotherapy Association. My son, Mike, asked me good questions, that helped me think through what to say and how to say it, and that was helpful. The people at New Harbinger were very helpful and cooperative, and special recognition is due to Catharine Sutker and Carole Honeychurch. Finally, nothing would be written without the cooperation of my husband, Wilford. To one and all, I say thank you very much.

Chapter 1

Who Are the Destructive Narcissists?

Do many of the following words or phrases fit a particular person or persons at your work site? If so, you may be unsuccessfully trying to cope with someone who has a destructive narcissistic pattern (DNP). Words or phrases that fit a DNP include:

- arrogant,
- takes unearned credit,
- constantly boasts and brags,
- has to be the center of attention,
- has an entitlement attitude,
- expects favors,
- demands preferential treatment,
- lacks empathy but can fake it,
- turns every conversation to self,
- arouses fury and confusion,
- never accepts responsibility for mistakes,
- grandiose,
- basks in reflected status,
- has a superior attitude.

Focus on the Workplace

Focusing on the workplace is important, as our work is a very significant part of our existence. For most everyone, work is necessary for survival and, for many, their work contributes to their self-concept and helps define who they are. There is considerable evidence that relationships in the workplace with peers or colleagues, bosses, and subordinates are a very important part of job satisfaction and motivation. When any of these relationships are unsatisfactory it leads to more general and personal dissatisfaction.

The person described as having a destructive narcissistic pattern in this book can be found in every setting and from all walks of life. They are everywhere, but you and others may not recognize them as destructive narcissists. They have succeeded in many ways, such as:

- becoming educated,
- attaining promotions,
- being placed in positions of responsibility,
- gaining acceptance as experts, and/or
- making considerable amounts of money.

This success must be recognized and remembered because they reached their present status and level in some way. They were able to navigate whatever system they were in and rise to their present level. They may have few talents or little expertise, but they have convinced others of their competence and abilities. Some material in this book may explain how they achieved their success, but an important point for the reader to remember is that they were indeed successful.

What Is a Destructive Narcissist?

The definition for destructive narcissism assumes that there is age-appropriate, healthy adult narcissism at one end of a continuum and pathological narcissism at the other end. Pathological narcissism is described as a collection of attitudes and behaviors that are troubling to others and to relationships and are described in the *Diagnostic and Statistical Manual of Mental Disorders* (2000). The pathological narcissist lacks meaningful, satisfying, and long-lasting relationships, creativity, empathy, and an appropriate sense of humor. At the other end of the continuum is healthy adult narcissism characterized by empathy, creativity, acceptance of personal responsibility, the ability to delay gratification, a recognition of personal boundaries and those of others, an appropriate sense of humor, and the ability to form and maintain meaningful and satisfying relationships.

Between the two extremes of pathological and healthy narcissism for adults is a large area where narcissism is underdeveloped. This is the area that encompasses stable and destructive narcissism. Stable is close to the healthy adult narcissism end of the continuum, and destructive is close to the pathological end. Since there are clusters of behaviors and attitudes that define narcissism and since people vary in the extent to which they have, display, and act on these behaviors and attitudes, there can be considerable underdevelopment of healthy adult narcissism. When there is considerable underdeveloped adult narcissism, this is termed a destructive narcissistic pattern. When there are few behaviors and attitudes descriptive of destructive narcissism and many behaviors reflective of healthy adult narcissism, this is termed stable narcissism. These descriptions are provided to keep you from viewing narcissism as an undesirable trait, as there is a need to develop healthy adult narcissism (Brown 1998).

Further, it's helpful to remember as you read this book that I'm not attempting to diagnose anyone. I'm simply providing a description to better understand why a work relationship may be unsatisfying and why you react and feel the way you do when you have to interact with him or her. There are several forms in later chapters to help you assess whether you may be dealing with a destructive narcissist at your workplace.

Behaviors and Attitudes of a DNP

This book extends the description of destructive narcissists and focuses on their presence in the workplace. The intents and purposes for the book are to increase awareness of this pattern in colleagues and bosses, suggest coping strategies, and to assist the reader in reviewing personal behaviors and attitudes that may be reflective of lingering aspects of their personal underdeveloped narcissism.

The term "destructive narcissist" was developed to describe the person who has a set of characteristics that contribute to destruction of relationships. Destructive narcissists seem unable to develop and maintain long-term, satisfying relationships in any part of their lives. They marry or enter many intimate relationships, but these do not last. In the workplace, this person may appear to have personally satisfying relationships, but if you looked more closely at their history and current situation, you'd most likely see that they only have these relationships with someone who can be of service to them or whom they consider to be of higher status.

The destructive narcissist:

- has contempt for those they consider inferior to themselves,
- constantly blames others for their mistakes,
- deliberately lies or withholds information
- has an attitude of superiority,
- takes unearned credit for ideas and accomplishments of others,
- boasts and brags,
- refocuses attention to themselves almost always,
- belittles others,
- makes devaluing and disparaging remarks to others,
- orders and directs others,
- frequently triggers feelings of frustration and confusion in interactions with others,
- does not respect rights and possessions of others,
- lacks empathy,
- is not creative,
- does not laugh or have a sense of humor, except to poke fun at others,
- demands that others defer to him or her,
- ignores rules and regulations,
- inflates their accomplishments,
- expects others to do favors for them but doesn't do favors in return,
- will lie, distort, and mislead,
- has a very limited range of emotional expression,
- uses others to meet their personal needs,
- feels that others are responsible for their emotional well-being, and
- cannot develop and maintain long-term, satisfying relationships.

These are not all of the behaviors and attitudes that describe a destructive narcissistic pattern, but they do represent a sample of behaviors that are part of the categories that define destructive narcissism. These categories are:

- a sense of entitlement,
- grandiosity,
- wanting to envied and admired,
- a lack of empathy,
- needing to be considered unique and special,
- considering others to be extensions of self, and
- needing to be the center of attention (Brown 1998).

Think of the behaviors and attitudes in this list as constellations or clusters that are habitual for the person and not isolated, unique events. That is, almost everyone at some time or other could behave or have an attitude that is grandiose or lacking in empathy. Unless they exhibit those clusters of attitudes and behaviors consistently, it doesn't necessarily mean that they have a destructive narcissistic pattern. They may have some underdeveloped aspect of narcissism, but could not be characterized as having a destructive narcissistic pattern.

There are two key indicators for a destructive narcissistic pattern:

- the inability to develop and maintain long-term, satisfying relationships and
- the ability to arouse intense, uncomfortable emotions, like anger and frustration in many people who must interact with them on a regular basis.

How Do You Feel Around a Destructive Narcissist?

You probably are in touch with your current feelings about the person that you think may have a destructive narcissistic pattern. You may have interacted with them over time but did not realize just how strong some of these unpleasant feelings were until you found that you were constantly angry, frustrated, or upset. These feelings did not happen all at once, but grew over a period of time. What generally happens is that people go through stages of reactions until they reach the point where merely thinking about the person arouses intense emotions. No matter how much you try to overlook, minimize, or shut down your feelings, you are unable to do so. But first, let's try to understand how these uncomfortable emotions developed.

Stages of reactions to a destructive narcissist suggest why it takes time for you to realize that you are trying to cope with someone who is not simply occasionally annoying, but has a serious problem like a destructive narcissistic pattern. You are not likely to be able to identify this pattern until you have observed and interacted with this person over a period of time, and even then you may not be sure. You just know that there is something awry. Stages are one way to think about the process of becoming aware of the destructive narcissistic pattern through an examination of your reactions to that person. But let me add a note of caution: Your reactions can be the result of your personal, unresolved issues and personality, not what the other person is doing or saying. The way to verify your identification is by group consensus. That is, find out if others are experiencing similar reactions to the person. If they are, then you can proceed to consider that you are dealing with destructive narcissism.

Consider the four stages below: the initial stage, the discomfort stage, the frustration stage, and the attack/avoidance stage. Table 1-1 presents some common reactions for each stage.

Table 1-1: Common Reactions to the Destructive Narcissist at Each Stage

Stage	Reactions
Stage 1: Initial	You're charmed, and develop a liking for the person; you're pleased and impressed.
Stage 2: Discomfort	You begin to experience generalized and nonspecific discomfort, irritation, and anxiety when dealing with the person.
Stage 3: Frustration	You're frequently frustrated, confused and annoyed with the person. Elements of self-doubt begin to emerge. You experience dread, fear, anger, and constant frustration when faced with the person.
Stage 4: Attack/Avoidance	You use attack or avoidance as a defense.

The Initial Stage

Destructive narcissists can be very charming and socially adept. When you first meet them they are likely to appear interested in you and go out of their way to let you know it. They listen to you, flatter you, and seem to hang on your every word. Who wouldn't like that? And since you have no other basis on which to react, you will probably react by liking the person and responding positively to them.

It's also likely that they are seeking someone to mirror or reflect their inflated self-perception, and new acquaintances are good candidates for this task. After all, who can resist giving a positive response to someone who seems to consider you irresistible and enchanting? They present themselves in a way that appears to reflect your more positive characteristics. You, in turn, reflect their self-perception by responding to them as being charming and superior—superior in the sense that you do not respond to others as positively as you respond to them.

They do not make devaluing or disparaging comments about you, although they may make these comments about others to you. You will probably ignore these comments about others or even agree with them, if you have similar perceptions of those people. You may spend time with the person, ask their opinion about things, do favors for them, and be very understanding of their problems or concerns. You do not really notice that much or all of this is one-way, and that you're not receiving any favors or understanding in return.

Stage 2: Discomfort

This stage emerges gradually. You probably are not consciously aware of any discomfort and, if you should become aware of being uncomfortable or irritated, you quickly dismiss it. You may even chide yourself for not being understanding or of letting your personal concerns get in the way. One difficulty is that both of these self-criticisms may be partially true. There may be times when you find yourself less understanding of the other person. You may be distracted, or maybe you're using distraction as a defense mechanism. There can also be personal concerns that keep you more focused on yourself than on others.

You begin to notice that the person has become less attentive to you. They no longer find excuses to be with you but still seem pleased when you're there. They don't listen as closely and will interrupt or change the topic. If you try to discuss a personal concern with them, you are likely to find that somehow the discussion winds up focusing on them. They may borrow things from you but do not return them, and they do not lend you anything.

You may begin to notice, without concern or alarm, that they will make negative comments about someone to you but go out of their way to flatter that person in a public setting. For example, they may complain that the boss is too dictatorial, but in a meeting they will tell the boss how much they appreciate his or her strong leadership, saying that the unit would not be as productive if anyone else was in the position.

You probably will not be consciously aware that the relationship with the destructive narcissist has shifted to stage 2 until the stage is almost over. Then you may recognize it only in retrospect. You may tend to rationalize any discomfort you have, but most people are more likely to suppress it. After all, you did find the person to be charming at one time and others still seem to find them charming.

Stage 3: Frustration

This stage brings your feelings about the person into sharper focus. You can no longer deny the uncomfortable feelings experienced in many, or all, interactions with the person. It may take you some time to realize and admit that you are generally left churned up after talking with them, but the feelings have become too intense and occur too often to be minimized or denied.

The reactions of many people at this point are to become self-critical and self-doubting. There are people who are introspective and keenly aware of what they consider to be personal flaws and failings. They care about others and work to develop and maintain relationships. They wind up asking themselves what *they* are doing that makes the destructive narcissist feel as they seem to and say the things they say. They want to know how they failed the person and the relationship. They ponder over what they could do to make the relationship better or return it to what it was when they first met.

In many relationships with a destructive narcissist, people begin to question their competencies and abilities. They are willing to accept and admit that they make mistakes, and when the destructive narcissist blames or accuses them, they wonder if the person is correct and they are indeed at fault. This kind of situation can really erode self-confidence.

Considerable confusion can also emerge, especially since destructive narcissists are prone to distort, mislead, and outright lie. However, these people are unlikely to admit any errors when they are pointed out to them. They are much more likely to turn it back on you and insist that you misunderstood. For example, they will give you incorrect information, and when you tell them the information was wrong, they maintain that you did not get your facts straight, and they did not say what you know you heard them say. If someone else heard them and verifies that you are correct, they may even accuse both of you of lying or of being wrong.

Stage 3 may linger for some time if you do not have to frequently interact with the destructive narcissist. However, if interactions are frequent, stage 4 quickly emerges.

Stage 4: Attack/Avoidance

As noted in table 1-1, feelings experienced during this stage are most unpleasant. Your behaviors become either those that are attacking or you simply find ways to avoid the person. You may find that you're acting in other ways that are uncharacteristic.

It's not unusual for people to find that they are angry, frustrated, or have a headache or upset stomach after interactions with the destructive narcissist. More troubling for most everyone is that they are not able to easily let go of these feelings, which persist for some time. This is particularly distressing if you are usually the type of individual who can get angry or upset, but who moderates relatively quickly and rarely obsesses over whatever happened. However, with the destructive narcissist you find that the feelings linger for a very long time and are reignited each time you have to interact with that person, or sometimes, even just by the prospect of having to interact. All these feelings are indications that you are in stage 4 of the relationship.

You may fantasize "getting rid" of the person. You devoutly wish that they would disappear, go somewhere else, or get out of your world in some way. You may find that you have to clench your fists and walk away from interactions with them because you are so angry. Other reactions may be those of aggression, wishes for their destruction, attempts or wishes that you could leave and never see them again, etc. If you are so inclined, you may cry from frustration.

You may find that you dread interactions so much that you go out of your way to avoid seeing or talking to the destructive narcissist. Your avoidance is a way of protecting yourself from feelings of:

- impotence,

- fury or rage,

- intense frustration, and/or

- a sense of losing control of yourself or of the situation.

This person seems to have an uncanny ability to trigger intense uncomfortable emotions that are not easily forgotten or ameliorated.

If you choose to attack, you will find that you experience the same level and intensity of feelings as those who choose to avoid do. At first you may attack because your previous experience was that the best defense is a good offense. You probably were successful in overcoming negativity in others with attacking and think that this will also work with the destructive narcissist. Wrong! What you're likely to find is that attacks are unsuccessful. The destructive narcissist is neither defeated nor changed and you are still left with your unpleasant feelings. An additional outcome may be the negative perceptions of you that others adopt because of your attacking behavior. While they may experience the destructive narcissist in the same way as you do, they are frightened by your attacking behavior and end up rejecting it and you.

There are other side effects for the reactions of attack or avoidance, ones that affect your attitudes and perceptions of self and of others and those that affect your behavior. You can begin to be suspicious, wary, and mistrustful of others and begin to isolate yourself. Worse, you can increase doubts about your competence, efficacy, and worth. These are interrelated and can happen when you don't fully understand what impact the person with a DNP has on you.

To give you some idea of just how powerful the impact of a person with a DNP can be I only have to think about the reactions and responses of everyone I've talked to about the concept of destructive narcissism. People immediately identify someone who fits the description and, no matter how many years ago they interacted with this person, are able to experience some of the same feelings of frustration and anger they had at that time. The impact of the destructive narcissist is powerful and lingers.

Impact on You

The immediate impact on the person who has to continually interact with a destructive narcissist is also powerful. That person's behaviors and attitudes and your responses can influence your self-perception and self-esteem even if you attempt to suppress any negative impact. You can try all of your usual strategies, such as ignoring how you feel, thinking that you can change the other person, and working harder to please that person.

However, what you will find is that these are not as effective with this person as they are with others. You can judge their effectiveness by the extent to which you are better able to tolerate interactions with the person. The defense may work for a while, or may easily be breached. That is, the defense does not protect you from experiencing those unpleasant feelings. You may unexpectedly find yourself continuing to question your abilities and competencies, even if you managed to defend against the unpleasant feelings. You may think that you are suppressing them or defending against them in some way, but the impact is still there and having a negative influence on your self-esteem.

Impact on Work Relationships

A very serious negative outcome can be on your relationships, both at work and with family and friends. Your struggle has its consequences and, unless you are aware of what the impact and your subsequent behavior is, these consequences do not have a positive contribution to strengthening and maintaining relationships. You may not become aware of the negative impact on other relationships until they are already damaged.

Possible impacts at work can be:

- a heightening of mistrust for fellow workers,
- increased irritability,
- taking offense easily,
- withdrawal from sociable interactions, and
- lessening of sympathy and concern for coworkers' problems and difficulties.

What can be devastating for a work unit is when almost all, or all, the members have these reactions to the impact of a destructive narcissist in their midst. When relationships are negatively impacted this way, creativity, productivity, and cooperation also suffer. Blaming, criticisms, and defensiveness become more common, and morale becomes low.

Impact on Personal Relationships

The possible impact on your personal life can follow much the same pattern as above but with more serious outcomes. These outcomes are more serious because they affect intimate relationships that make up your vital support system. We derive considerable succor and encouragement from our intimate relationships, which also greatly influence our self-perceptions and self-esteem. The people you're in these relationships with are generally unable to understand why you're acting differently, especially when you do not understand it yourself. You may describe the person with a DNP and your feelings about them but cannot explain why you react as you do and why you cannot let go of the feelings. Your loved ones can observe that you are still mired in the aroused, unpleasant feelings when generally you are able to shrug off these kinds of events and feelings, but they remain puzzled about all of it.

If you try to separate workplace concerns from the rest of your life, you can find that trying to do so has an unanticipated outcome. What can happen is that you unconsciously displace the feelings and reactions that result from interactions with a destructive narcissist on your family and friends. You probably are not aware of what you're doing, and they can't understand your behavior because you are choosing not to talk about your experiences at work. You may find that you:

- exhibit more general irritability,

- are more anxious,

- become quicker to criticize or blame others,

- are impatient,

- tend to be more easily offended or angered,

- become unrealistic in your expectations for perfection in self and others,

- show defensiveness at the least hint of perceived criticism, even when none is meant, and

- are less empathic.

Those nearest and dearest to you cannot help but be affected and puzzled.

What's in the Rest of the Book

The remainder of the book presents material to help you identify someone with a destructive narcissist pattern at work. This person may be a colleague, a boss, or a worker whom you supervise. I also will provide you with powerful coping strategies. A variety of strategies are suggested so that you can pick and choose those that best fit your personality and work situation, as each is unique. The best use for the suggested strategies is to trigger your creativity in developing your own coping mechanisms. The final part of the book focuses on helping you develop stronger boundaries and manage unpleasant feelings that are triggered by the destructive narcissist.

You may want to deny or not admit that you, too, may have some underdeveloped narcissism. How could that be? You are not like the person you identified as a destructive narcissist! You may be right, but even then you may still have areas of underdeveloped narcissism that affect you negatively. One important point to keep in mind is that people with a destructive narcissistic pattern are blind to their behavior and attitudes. They simply cannot see or be aware of the destructive nature of what they're doing or of their basic assumptions. They consider themselves to be justified and right in their behavior and attitudes. Further, they think that everyone else is like them. We may be similar in our inability to perceive our underdeveloped areas of narcissism. Hence, the final portion of the book, chapters 9 and 10, will help you to identify and develop these areas in yourself.

Read the final portion with the openness to consider that you may have some growing and developing to do. Even if you do need to change, you don't have to make massive changes all at once. You can experiment with small changes in behaviors over time and become more aware of the impact of your behaviors and attitudes. What is important is that you increase your awareness. That, in itself, is growth.

Chapter 2

The Narcissistic Coworker

Interacting with a coworker who has a destructive narcissistic pattern can be especially difficult because you generally have to work with them on a frequent or daily basis. Coworkers are mainly peers, and it is helpful when there can be mutual respect, cooperation, and trust between you. When destructive narcissism enters the picture, all three go out of the window and in their place are a lack of respect, the kind of competition that invites aggression and subterfuge, and considerable distrust. Instead of interdependence and teamwork, there is backbiting and considerable hugger-mugger in the environment.

It may take you some time before you can identify what it is about a colleague that makes you uncomfortable, and at first you may be inclined to attribute any discomfort to a basic personality clash with the person. You may even feel that you are the only one to experience them this way and try very hard to overcome your feelings and smooth over any friction. If your colleague has some, but not numerous, behaviors and attitudes indicative of destructive narcissism, it may take even longer to come to the conclusion that they have these traits and to accept that you must learn to cope with them.

The behaviors and attitudes listed in table 2-1 are some of the major ones that are associated with destructive narcissism in coworkers. There are also some overlapping characteristics with those presented for the destructive narcissistic boss found in chapter 4. The following items focus on the coworkers.

Table 2-1: The Self-Absorbed Coworker

Directions: Select a coworker with whom you experience conflict or are unable to have a cooperative work relationship. Rate the extent to which he or she exhibits each of the following behaviors and attitudes using the following scale.

5 - Almost always	2 - Seldom
4 - Frequently	1 - Never or almost never
3 - Sometimes	0 - Does not apply

 1. Inflates accomplishments

 2. Always has all the answers

 3. Devalues the work of others

 4. Gives you and/or others work without authority to do so

 5. Expects you to do personal favors

 6. Takes credit for others' work

 7. Interrupts you and others

 8. Expects you to stop what you're doing and attend to them

 9. Disparages input from others

10. Talks about doing but does little

11. Does not knock before entering your office or workplace; uses your possessions without asking permission

12. Does not wait for an invitation to enter or sit down in your space

13. Lie, cheats, distorts, misleads

14. Overreacts to perceived criticism

15. Lacks creativity or originality but trashes or co-opts ideas of others

Total _____

Now add the numbers you checked and total them. Use the guide below to identify the destructive narcissistic colleague.

60–75   Has many destructive narcissistic behaviors and attitudes

45–59   Has considerable destructive narcissistic behaviors and attitudes

30–44 Has some destructive narcissistic behaviors and attitudes

15–29 Has few behaviors or attitudes that tend to make working relationships difficult

0–14 Has no behaviors or attitudes indicative of destructive narcissism

Descriptions and Illustrations of Items

The behaviors and attitudes in table 2-1 are not exhaustive but are examples of common workplace actions that take place between coworkers. It is not possible to include all behaviors and attitudes, and some (like attacks others), were not included at this point so that the more insidious destructive narcissistic behaviors and attitudes would remain in focus. These are the actions that make you and others question this person's abilities, competencies, etc. Many of the behaviors and attitudes cannot be openly and directly challenged, as the challenger may then appear to be picking on the other person or overreacting. For example, if you tell a coworker that he or she talks about doing things but, in reality, does very little, you may be correct in your observation. But you will probably get little support from your other coworkers, and you run the risk of being perceived as unnecessarily negative toward the person. Everyone else may have the same opinion but do not see that anything useful comes out of your confronting or telling them. In one instant you can alienate or negatively impact all your workplace relationships. The fact that you are correct is often of no help.

When the coworker has a pattern or constellation of behaviors and attitudes that suggest destructive narcissism (as described in table 2-1), you may find that you feel relieved at the identification. You knew that you were often uncomfortable, frustrated, and/or angry after interactions with the person, but the specific behaviors and attitudes that produced those feelings did not seem severe enough to warrant your reactions. This is what often happens with destructive narcissists—they have a collection of behaviors and attitudes that seem on the surface to not warrant the produced reaction. It is only when their behaviors and attitudes are combined with your and others' feelings that you realize that you are dealing with a destructive narcissist. The realization only develops over time.

The following descriptions and illustrations may help identify what I mean by destructive narcissism. You may also want to do a self-rating to see which descriptions fit your personal behaviors and attitudes, and/or for which you have received criticism.

Inflates Accomplishments

This behavior indicates a need to be the center of attention and a deep desire for admiration. This item describes a coworker who regularly is exhibitionistic, brags, and uses self-aggrandizement. They never seem to just do anything, they DO THINGS! Not only that, they puff up whatever they do but do not seem to realize that coworkers may find this behavior offensive. They may also assume that others do the same and so are very ready to disparage the accomplishments of others.

A good example of this behavior occurred in a university where a professor sent a copy of his recent publication around to colleagues with the note that they should read his article because it was ground-breaking and of national importance. It turned out that the article was a good one, but not especially noteworthy or groundbreaking. He became offended when one colleague told him that he would do well to let others praise him instead of engaging in self-praise. It should also be noted that this was not the first time this professor had exaggerated his accomplishments, but usually no one called him on it.

Always Has All the Answers

Some people seem to have all the answers and are not reluctant to share them with everyone—whether or not they are asked. When you work with someone like this it can get to be very annoying because not only do they seem to know all the answers, they do not seem to feel that anyone else could possibly know as much as they do or be correct as often as they are. They tend to be arrogant, over-bearing, and have an exaggerated sense of self-importance.

Have you ever noticed that some adults tend to relate to new experiences in terms of their old experiences? Children do this because of their lack of experience. When adults do it, it's an imma-ture response. Children and immature adults cannot see that the new situation or thing may have different characteristics. Whereas many other people may try to see similarities between the old and the new, they remain aware that the new will have some different characteris-tics. The person with a DNP will not be able to discern or acknowl-edge any differences from their experience. This is one of the reasons why the individual who has all the answers will begin many of their statements with the words "In my experience . . .". Even when some-one points out differences to them, they will discount or ignore what is different.

It is very grandiose to assume that you know all the answers or that you know what is "best." This attitude also points to an inflated sense of self-importance that is associated with grandiosity. When you work with a someone who has this behavior and attitude, you may (understandably) find that you dread being in a meeting with them or having to interact with them at all.

Devalues the Work of Others

The coworker who devalues others' work:

- is trying to appear superior to others by tearing them down,
- has the assumption that he or she is unique and special and that others are not quite as good and deserving, and/or
- considers that he or she is the only competent one around.

Devaluing remarks can be made directly about or to others. It is not unusual for someone with this destructive narcissistic behavior to say something directly to an individual that is devaluing of them or of their work. Comments such as:

- "Got called on the carpet again, didn't you?"
- "You always seem to be in trouble,"
- "When are you going to start on your diet. You're really putting on the pounds," or
- "When are you going to get rid of that clunker you are driving?"

are examples of direct comments.

Indirect comments can be made in the presence of the person targeted or when they are absent. If the person is present, the intent is to make the devaluing comment so that everyone gets the message but also making certain that the speaker cannot be effectively challenged. If the person is absent, the intent is to get the listener to agree with and even add to the devaluing comment.

Gives Orders

Coworkers who give orders to their peers without really having any authority to do so consider themselves to be unique, special, and perfectly entitled to give the orders. They are usually somewhat grandiose in the assumption that they know better than others what needs to be done. These are the people who do not make requests of others—they make demands. They do not routinely use the words "please" and "thank you" to others, simply assuming that they will be obeyed.

If you encounter this behavior you may waste a lot of time and energy fretting about arrogance and high-handedness of these coworkers. You may confront them or resist actively, but this does not appear to change their behavior in any way.

Some people may not understand that their failure to use "please" and "thank you" comes across as giving an order. They unintentionally give offense by their abruptness. This is different from individuals who are arrogant when they give orders and have an entitlement attitude of expecting to be obeyed. It doesn't take very long to determine if the person is simply abrupt and isn't given to using a courteous manner, or is giving an order.

A person with this destructive narcissistic characteristic does not understand what others object to when they give an order. They feel that, because they do know what others ought to do and since they go to the trouble to make sure that person knows this, then the person ought to just go ahead and do what they were told. Needless to say, this attitude does not make for a comfortable working relationship.

Expects You to Do Personal Favors

You may unintentionally fall into the trap of doing personal favors for the coworker with a DNP, later finding that doing so has become an expectation instead of your having the choice. When you first arrive on the job or at the unit, you may want to be accepted and to feel a part of the group. So when you're asked to do personal favors, you will most likely go out of your way to comply. Or your personality may be such that you want to please others, and so you find yourself doing personal favors that may be inappropriate.

If you have a self-absorbed coworker, you will shortly become aware that not only are you expected to do personal favors for them, but they make it very clear that you should not expect reciprocity. You will be asked to do things such as run errands, finish work for them, collate papers, take telephone messages, and so on. However, if you should be so imprudent as to ask that coworker to do any-thing for you, they will most likely find some reason why they can-not do the favor for you.

You will have to weigh the costs and benefits of doing personal favors with no hope of any return. Your personal style may allow you to do so, and it may not bother you a bit. However, you need to be aware that others observe what is happening and will wonder why you allow yourself to be taken advantage of. They may even begin to feel that they can begin to take advantage themselves. You may also feel that it is not worth the hassle to refuse to do favors, or that it is better to go along with the expectations. Your personal style will also influence a decision not to do favors, especially after you find out there will be no reciprocity.

Takes Credit for Others' Work

A productive work environment cannot exist when there is suspicion, mistrust, deception, and lies among colleagues. If there is someone who takes credit for others' work, then all of these negative forces undermine any prospect for a cohesive productive group.

Even when the final product is a result of team effort there is still room for individual contributions, and each team member can receive some recognition for their particular effort. There are other situations where the person's work is the final product, and it is important that their work be recognized. In both instances, if credit is not appropriately given the end result is resentment and acrimony.

A self-absorbed coworker may routinely take credit for work done by others. For example, if there is a report where everyone in the unit or team had input and made contributions, the coworker with a DNP will submit the paper with only their name on it. In some instances, they may include a short note that others contributed, but none of their names will be included and the impression is given that the bulk of the work was done by that one person. Another example that may sound familiar is when you have developed an idea, discussed it with others or in a meeting, and then found that the idea has been presented by the destructive narcissist as if they were the author or originator. It is very disconcerting (to say the least) to hear your idea presented by someone else with no credit being given to you.

The self-absorbed coworker does not even recognize or accept that they are taking credit for others' work. If challenged, they defend taking the unearned credit by:

- ignoring others' contributions,
- disparaging coworkers' contributions,
- pointing out that they got there first, or
- conveniently forgetting that someone else presented the idea first.

They do this over and over.

The result is that considerable mistrust develops in the team or unit, a feeling that compromises creativity and productivity. Members become reluctant to discuss ideas, fearing that they will be stolen. Dialogue is stifled and members become more and more isolated. If group work is an integral part of the job, the cohesiveness needed to have good productivity is compromised. Both team members and managers become frustrated as the cause for lack of cohesiveness is not readily apparent. Concerns may not be openly discussed or addressed, but these issues and concerns continue to erode trust and safety.

Interrupts You and Others

Have you ever found yourself in a situation where you were having a conversation with someone and another individual walked up to you and blatantly interrupted? What did you do? How did you feel? Did you try to continue the conversation as if this person had not interrupted? Did you give them your attention and stop what you were doing? Was it possible to ignore him or her?

Politeness and respect for others would suggest that when you approach an existing conversation, you do so quietly, waiting for a break or some recognition before saying anything. Interrupting others is considered rude and shows a lack of respect. It is very interesting that those of higher status consider it appropriate for them to interrupt others but not the reverse unless the person interrupting is of higher status. This means that the boss feels free to interrupt workers but workers are not free to interrupt the boss. It also means that the coworker who feels free to interrupt peers may consider him or herself to be of higher status.

As you may know, it does become annoying when a coworker constantly interrupts whatever is going on and focuses the attention on him- or herself. Even when it's pointed out that they are interrupting, their response is apt to be something like, "Sorry," proceeding to continue talking about their concerns.

The coworker who fits this description may feel that they are of higher status than their peers and thus entitled to interrupt. They may also feel that unless the topic is of concern to them or about them that it was not important and should be changed—so they interrupt.

Expect Others to Attend to Them

Self-centered people expect others to drop what they are doing and immediately attend to their needs. Have you ever experienced a coworker who sees that you are busy but comes into your office and talks about their concerns anyway? Even if you say that you're busy but will get back to them when you are finished, they do not leave or stop talking. This person really expects you to drop what you are doing and attend to them. In their view, what they want is all-important.

Other ways that coworkers expect you to attend to them include:

- being sympathetic to their troubles and woes;
- sending cards, gifts, etc. when they are sick or for birthdays;
- seeing to it that they are not inconvenienced; and
- listening to them.

Some attending is to be expected if cordial relationships are to be developed. The work environment demands that coworkers listen to each other and be considerate. But what destructive narcissistic coworkers demand goes far beyond basic workplace expectations.

It may take some time before you accept that you're dealing with someone who has a destructive narcissistic pattern. You may find yourself annoyed, frustrated, and angry many times before realizing that the person is essentially self-centered and expects you to drop what you are doing and attend to him/her. You may become angry with yourself because you find yourself doing what these self-absorbed people expect and putting their desires ahead of your needs. Their priorities may begin taking the place of your priorities, and you are agreeing with their attitude by your behavior. When you realize that you are doing this, you may begin to berate yourself.

Disparages Input from Others

Arrogance, grandiosity, and a sense of superiority describe the coworker who routinely disparages input from others. It's not uncommon to find that there is someone in the unit or on the team who does not have good ideas or who can be counted on to get confused. While no one will openly disparage this person's input, there can be tacit agreement that their input will be ignored, as it is apt to be misleading. However, the destructive narcissist will disparage input from everyone, assuming that he or she is the only one who is competent and able to have informed contributions.

For example, you may find that there is someone who finds fault or makes disparaging remarks about any suggestions, ideas, proposed solutions, etc., suggested by others. The only ideas this person does not find fault with are the ones they propose. It does not appear to make a difference that other team members find merit in some suggestions because the destructive narcissist does not consider other team members capable of exercising good judgment. Self-absorbed people assume that they are the only ones who have the necessary ability and know-how to develop meaningful and work-able ideas, solutions, and suggestions.

Working with someone like this can be very demoralizing, as self-absorbed people are very open in their contempt for others. They make sarcastic, cutting remarks that are designed to put the other person on the defensive and to show that the self-absorbed person is superior. This gets to be aggravating after a while, and some cowork-ers may begin to doubt their competence.

Talks but Doesn't Act

In addition to bragging and inflating their accomplishments, coworkers with destructive narcissism will talk about doing but, in reality, do very little. Their accomplishments are shallow and mea-ger. If you were to listen and believe what they say, you would come away with the conviction that this person is a tireless worker and that nothing constructive would ever be accomplished without them. But, in fact, the person contributes little to the accomplishments of the group and is blowing hot air.

For example, a coworker is given the assignment of gathering data, analyzing it, and writing a report. This person talks about the task and what they intend to do about it at every opportunity, sug-gesting that they are in the middle of carrying out these actions. However, when the report is submitted, none or very few of these things were done. The report is very meager, poorly presented, and of no consequence.

Another example is when this kind of coworker talks about their extensive network and how this will enable them to bring in more accounts than anyone else. These accounts never materialize.

The academic world has many of these self-absorbed people. They may never publish very much, although to hear them talk, no one in the world publishes as much as they do. They claim that they cannot participate in other tasks because they must spend their time on publishing their very important work. They constantly talk about how much work they do, but an objective analysis would show that they teach fewer students, do less administrative work, write fewer reports, and when they do write reports, the reports are unsatisfac-tory. However, they do talk an awful lot about what they're suppos-edly doing.

It can take some time before you realize that they are talking a lot but doing little, particularly when you do not routinely see the result. Gradually you become aware that this person is exaggerating and actually producing very little. Or you happen upon a copy of one of their reports and are shocked at how awful it is. Or perhaps you are assigned to work with him or her on a project, and you wind up with most of the work while they talk up their accomplishments and wind up with the credit. It may even take several of these events before you accept that this coworker, in fact, is not pulling their weight.

Accompanying this characteristic all too often is the boss's acceptance of this person's self-analysis. The boss believes that they did the work, that it was not their fault that the report is so meager, that others did not do what they were supposed to, etc. The self-absorbed worker's shortcomings are overlooked, explained away, or ignored. Colleagues can only marvel at their ability to exploit the situation.

Does Not Knock

Just like interrupting conversations with no regard for others, some coworkers have the habit of invading your workplace without asking for permission. These self-absorbed people think nothing of barging into your office or workplace without knocking and can become offended if you ask them to do so.

These are the same people who consider it their right to take or use your possessions without first asking. They will take your pens, papers, books, tools, and will even be found using your computer without your permission. It can be very awkward to ask someone not to take your paper clips, as this can seem petty. But this person can quickly move from taking paper clips to taking more expensive and valuable possessions. Just because your expensive fountain pen was a gift from someone special does not prevent them from assuming they are entitled to use it without first asking you.

Two destructive narcissistic characteristics are at work in these situations—entitlement and a lack of recognition of boundaries, where others are considered to be an extension of self. Some, if not all, destructive narcissists consider themselves to be unique and special, entitled to be treated better than others. They are convinced that they are not bound by the same rules and laws that govern others but can operate as they choose. The lack of recognition of boundaries occurs because others are considered by the destructive narcissist as an extension of self. This means that they fail to recognize where they end and others begin. They invade others' physical and psychological space because they cannot understand that others' are different from them. They consider, for example, that your office or workplace is theirs, and so they have a right to use it as they see fit. This attitude also explains some of their behavior in using or taking your possessions.

Does Not Wait for Invitations

There are coworkers who may knock, but do not wait for an invitation to enter or wait to be invited to sit. They just breeze in and sit with no concern about interrupting you. Some do not even seem to care if you already have a visitor and appear to be in a deep discussion.

You may have a close friend at work who will do this, and you may or may not be irritated when they behave this way. It all depends on your personality. However, it is simple courtesy for everyone, including friends and the boss, to not only knock but to wait for an invitation to enter and to sit down. When you enter someone's office and are comfortable with the person, you may still want to ask if they have time for you to sit and talk. The person may just be slow in extending an invitation, and at least you asked and did not assume it was okay to interrupt.

Few people are not bothered on some level by coworkers who do not wait for an invitation to enter or to be seated. It may only be a small flash of irritation or annoyance that is easily suppressed, ignored, or denied, but it's there. This behavior demonstrates a lack of respect for your boundaries and a lack of recognition of the coworker's differentiation from others. It also shows a lingering sense of entitlement, assuming that they have the right and power to go and sit anywhere they choose.

Lies, Distorts, Cheats, and Misleads

Most workplaces rely on cooperation and collaboration between workers and units to get the job done. Outcomes, especially effective, efficient, and productive outcomes, are enhanced and facilitated by the free and easy exchange of information, ideas, expertise, and so on. If the ideal of cooperation and collaboration is to be realized, then it is crucial that trust exist between workers, especially those who work on a team or in a unit. Coworkers need to be confident that each person can be relied on to give accurate and complete information, that there is an open and accepting atmosphere that encourages ideas from each, and that expertise is not withheld or denied. In short, they need to know that each person can be trusted.

This necessary situation is also true of very competitive workplace environments. While the degree of trust needed or expected may be different, the need still exists if the work for the unit is to be done. It is the rare place where only individual effort is rewarded and there are no expectations of the unit as a whole. For example, even in the highly competitive work of sales, there are expectations for the total sales volume for a dealership, a sales department, or an advertising agency. Individuals may be recognized and rewarded for having the highest sales volume but the overriding expectation is a high number of sales overall

It is for these and other important reasons that working with a coworker who lies, distorts, cheats, and/or deliberately misleads is detrimental to the working environment and to productivity. If you work with a destructive narcissist, he or she will do all those things. It takes time, but their coworkers learn that they cannot be relied on to be truthful, accurate, or honest in their dealings with others. This circumstance erodes trust, promotes secrecy and suspicion, and hampers productivity.

You may be familiar with this situation and have a coworker who is either a destructive narcissist or who has many of these behaviors. You may even have challenged them on occasion and pointed out that you knew they were not being truthful or were misleading. You probably tried to be tactful and give the person the benefit of the doubt by saying it in a way that makes the lie or misleading information seem as though it was done unintentionally. If you've tried this tactic, what probably occurred was not what you had anticipated, as the person refused to admit any error and turned it back on you in some way. They may have become angry and gone on the offensive, changed the subject in such a way that you could not continue the discussion without looking bad, or were so adamant that you backed down. This person's behavior then compounded the feelings generated by the lies, deception, cheating, or misleading: you feel misused, frustrated, and perhaps a bit bewildered.

These people use deception to manipulate others and to demonstrate their superiority. It is such an ingrained behavior and attitude that they do not perceive anything wrong in what they are doing. In some way, they feel entitled to exploit other people as everyone other than their own selves is deemed to be less worthy and deserving.

The most distressing thing about this situation is that there is nothing you can do to get through to them. They may not lie all of the time, but they do so enough that everyone who deals with them is kept on edge, as they can never be sure when the person is telling the truth and when they're not. This state of affairs also erodes trust and impacts morale and productivity.

Overreacts to Perceived Criticism

Have you ever worked with someone who never admitted to making a mistake, was never wrong about anything, and who managed to blame others for whatever was not correct? This is the person who is usually oversensitive to perceived criticism and who will mount a vigorous defense at the slightest hint of criticism, even when none was intended.

These people infer criticism from almost anything. If you point out how well someone is doing, they take it as criticism that they are not doing as well. If a question is asked of this person about a point they've made, they can become defensive, because the fact that a question is asked suggest that they were not perfectly clear or have made an error. They are quick to attack when they think they are being criticized or blamed, and they feel this way quite often.

They may also be perfectionists and have standards that neither they nor anyone else can meet. They are dissatisfied with their inability to live up to what they want to be and displace much of this dissatisfaction onto others. They may be fearful that others see their failings and so take aggressive steps to make sure that others know that they are perfect and do not make mistakes.

These behaviors and attitudes make these people very difficult to work with, and coworkers become tentative and careful in their dealings with them in order to prevent attacks. It's always very difficult to work with someone who is quick to take offense and see criticism where none is intended.

Lacks Creativity

A lack of creativity and originality is a characteristic found in destructive narcissists. This state is usually coupled with the habit or tendency to disparage creativity and originality in others. Coworkers who are not creative or original can have other valuable abilities and expertise that contribute to satisfying workplace relationships and productivity, so it's not just the lack of creativity and originality that makes those with destructive narcissism uncomfortable with their more creative coworkers. For self-absorbed people, it is a nonconscious awareness that they lack creativity and are jealous of others' creativity that makes them uncomfortable.

These are the people who can bring up so many objections to any idea or proposal that the presenter or developer begins to wish he or she had never said anything. The objections may be couched in terms such as, "Have you thought about . . . ?" "How do you propose to . . . ?" "Did you take into consideration . . . ?" On the surface, these may appear to be legitimate questions and, indeed, may need to be addressed. But if the person asks a lot of these types of questions about most every suggestion or idea, and especially with an air of disdain or disapproval, the person is generally trying to disparage the idea.

These are also the people who are at a loss for constructive suggestions when asked. They tend to stick to what has been tried before with no adaptations for the present, whether or not it was successful in the past or has sufficient application for the present. It can get to the point where their coworkers dread bringing up a problem, concern, or new initiative because their destructive narcissistic coworker will waste time tearing it apart without contributing anything new.

The destructive narcissist does not understand creativity or the creative process. Creativity is a characteristic of healthy narcissism in adults, and these people have not developed to this point. Just like small children, they tend to discount anything outside their own experience, although the adult destructive narcissist does it in an aggressive, attacking way. Children would tend to ignore it, but these adults feel threatened by anything they do not understand.

Summary

The destructive narcissistic pattern of characteristics I've presented and described in this chapter does not cover the full range of their behaviors and attitudes. For many of these traits, my brief descriptions and examples cannot begin to convey the corrosive nature of these behaviors and attitudes on their coworkers, the workplace environment, and the quality of work produced.

As you review the behaviors and attitudes, you may wish to reflect on which ones could also be descriptive of you. You may be aware that you behave in some of these ways or have these attitudes but be unaware of the impact on your coworkers. Just as the destructive narcissist remains unaware of his or her behaviors and attitudes that are distressing to others, so may we remain unaware of our possible destructive narcissistic characteristics. Being open to reflection on our possible destructive narcissistic behaviors and attitudes gives us an opportunity to grow and develop more healthy narcissism.

Chapter 3 presents some suggested strategies for coping with destructive narcissistic coworkers.

Chapter 3

Coping with the Destructive Narcissistic Coworker

You Are Not Helpless

Once you are confident that your coworker is very likely a destructive narcissist, your next task is to develop and use strategies to help you cope with their troubling behavior and manage your unpleasant emotions. This chapter presents some suggested strategies to use with a coworker, assuming that you do not have the option of leaving that particular environment at this point.

The primary strategy is to realize that you are not helpless. There are actions you can take and attitudes you can assume that can help moderate the impact of the self-absorbed coworker's behavior on you. As you read through the strategies, evaluate them as possibilities and how, or if, you could use them. You will want to use those that are consistent with your personality, and comfortable for you, and do not violate your perception of how you should behave.

Review the strategies and reflect on how you felt when others used them on you. For example, you may have experienced someone refusing to stop what they were doing and attend to you. How did you feel when that happened? Were you understanding because you interrupted when they were engrossed in what they were doing? Or did you feel the person was rude not to drop everything because you were there and wanted attention? Did you feel discounted? As you reflect on your feelings, you may gain a heightened awareness of the impact of your behavior on others. Do not make the mistake of thinking that your reactions are the same that a destructive narcissist would have. For the most part, they do not have the same reactions as do many others because of their sense of entitlement and grandiosity. They are immune to honestly evaluating their feelings or the impact of their behavior and attitudes.

Decisions about the Relationship

Before implementing any suggested strategies, first make a decision about what you want for your relationship with the self-absorbed coworker.

- Do you want a distant, cold relationship?
- Do you want the self-absorbed coworker to accept and like you?
- Do you want to maintain harmony at all costs?
- Do you want a cordial and professional relationship?
- Do you want to put them in their place?
- Do you want to be friends and socialize with them?

Your needs are very important in making a decision about which strategies to use.

They Will Not Change

What you will have to accept is that the destructive narcissistic coworker will not change because you want him or her to, and that all your efforts to get them to truly understand the impact of their behavior on you are doomed to failure. These self-absorbed people will discount your concerns as not really having anything to do with them. You cannot get through to them, and the more you try to, the more frustrated and angry you become. They remain detached, and you end up with all the pain.

When you can accept that the destructive narcissist will not change, then your decision becomes one of choosing strategies that you can implement effectively and that are most consistent with your personality and values. You do have choices. You can choose to keep the relationship as harmonious as possible and give in to their demands and orders just to get along; you can stand your ground and be eternally vigilant to make sure they do not take advantage of you; you can let your feelings be known in direct and indirect ways. It is also possible to go on the offensive and be aggressive. There are numerous possibilities, and you can use strategies that are consistent with your needs and with the situation.

Attitudes to Adopt

There are a few attitudes and expectations that will be helpful. Perhaps it will be difficult at first to accept some of them, but they can be helpful.

- Expect the self-absorbed coworker to mislead you.
- Expect that they will cheat.
- A professional, polite, somewhat cool relationship may be the most you can hope for.
- You do not have to respond to criticism or blame.
- You do not have to be perfect.
- Their approval is not necessary for your self-concept or well-being.
- Empathizing with them is futile.

Expectations

Expecting someone to mislead you, give erroneous information, lie, or cheat is not a pleasant frame of mind or attitude to assume. It is more comfortable to expect the best of others and to convince yourself that they may make mistakes, but that there is not evil intent.

However, when you are dealing with a destructive narcissist and you give them this much leeway, you will find yourself constantly being unpleasantly surprised at their lies and misleading information. Worse, there will be little or nothing you can do when you become aware of their deceptions. You will have acted on misleading or erroneous information, and no amount of explaining will absolve you from that responsibility. In addition, if you try to point out that you acted on information received from the destructive narcissist, they will deny giving you wrong information. What you end up with is a "he said/she said" situation. You end up looking worse.

Expecting these behaviors means that you do not totally rely on information received from this person, and you take steps to receive appropriate credit for your work or contribution. How you do this is discussed in the section called "Active Verbal Strategies."

You can prevent considerable dismay and reduce being upset by adapting to the reality that this person cannot be trusted to be accurate or fair. It really does not make any difference if their actions are intentional, unintentional, or with or without malice. You will take better care of yourself if you accept that you can expect these behaviors.

A Realistic Relationship

As noted before, you need to decide what you want from the relationship with the destructive narcissistic colleague. Your needs will determine what kind of relationship you will seek to develop and maintain. What may be possible is not necessarily what you want to have.

Coming to terms with what is realistic and what is a fantasy or dream is not easy. Most of us would like to have pleasant, cordial, trustworthy, friendly, and positive relationships with our colleagues. We want to work as a team where all members are:

- contributing,

- accepting and respectful of others,

- helpful,

- trusting and trustworthy,

- willing to share responsibilities and recognition, and

- open and genuine.

Under these circumstances, we will feel valued and be willing to work hard.

However, what we're faced with when working with a destructive narcissistic coworker are the opposites of the desirable conditions. This is one of the reasons why you need to be realistic about the quality of the relationship you can expect or establish.

One characteristic that will stand you in good stead is to be professional and to expect to have only a professional relationship with this coworker. A professional relationship means that you:

- do not give nor expect personal information,

- don't seek to socialize,

- limit conversations to professional matters,

- respect their boundaries and demand that yours receive respect,
- confine your remarks to professionally relevant material,
- do not gossip with them, and
- are pleasant and polite but nothing beyond that.

Take Care of Yourself

Your well-being is important for your health and your relationships. Until you realize that you are dealing with destructive narcissists and accept that you cannot change them, both your health and your relationships are likely to be negatively affected. The effects on you are gradual and cumulative and probably have affected parts of your life in ways you did not realize.

If you are tempted to invest more in the relationship with the coworker, try harder to get them to understand, or make excuses for their attitudes and behavior, you are headed toward becoming more frustrated, upset, and angry, which in turn has a negative effect on your well-being. Until you can accept that this person cannot or will not change and that you cannot effect this change, you will not take actions to insure your well-being.

How do you achieve this acceptance? You will find that you will have to constantly remind yourself that you cannot change them, that no matter what you do or say, they will not understand what you mean. They do not and cannot understand the impact of their behaviors and attitudes on others. You will also have to increase your awareness of what you are feeling and of the negative impact interactions with this person have on you. All of what you are experiencing is not that person's fault—you also have some responsibility. For example, if you continue to engage the self-absorbed coworker in conversation when every time you come away feeling upset, angry, frustrated, incompetent, etc., then your feelings are your responsibility. It's different if the coworker is the one to initiate conversations. You'll have different strategies for that. However, if you are the initiator, then you are helping to keep yourself upset, frustrated, etc. Make a resolution to take better care of yourself.

You Don't Have to Respond

The usual tendency is to give a response (denial, explanation, etc.) when blamed or criticized. After all, you do not want the person to have the wrong impression of you or of what happened. You may even accept some or all of the responsibility, feel guilty or ashamed, or want to correct any mistakes.

It will be difficult for you to change your characteristic way of responding, but you will find that you are much better off if you can train yourself not to respond to any blame or criticism from the destructive narcissistic coworker.

Does the suggestion to not respond sound rude to you? For some people, not responding is considered rude, and most people do not want to appear rude. But when you are dealing with a destructive narcissist, you may need to make a priority of protecting yourself. What you will find is that you are contributing to your own distress by trying to counter, challenge, or explain when blamed or criticized by the destructive narcissist. It's better to simply avoid engaging.

Lock these words in your mind: **You do not have to respond to blame or criticism.** Not responding means just that—you make no response. Just look at the person, leave, or change the subject, but do not respond. You are not being rude. *They* were rude to make these comments. You are just ignoring their rudeness.

Give Yourself a Break

Albert Ellis developed a therapy strategy called Rational Emotive Therapy or RET. One premise of this theory is that we cause ourselves distress with our irrational beliefs; for example, making ourselves and others miserable, believing that we must be perfect. This is one irrational belief that causes people to engage in considerable self-blame, self-chastisement, guilt, and shame. If you tend to have this belief, having to work with a destructive narcissist gives you considerable opportunities to find out just how flawed you are and have all your feelings about the need to be perfect triggered.

Go ahead and give yourself permission to:

- make mistakes,
- be wrong,
- be good enough, and
- not feel guilty about your lack of perfection.

Don't Pursue Their Approval

Your self-concept is influenced in part by how others react to and treat you. This is true for almost everyone—we all want to have others' approval.

However, wanting approval is not the same as *seeking* approval. Just how far are you willing to go to gain the approval you seek? Are you willing to let them say or do things that make you uncomfortable or upset, take advantage of your good nature, or just generally jerk you around? Do you find yourself wondering how you let someone do these things to you? You are seeking approval when you let others decide for you, take advantage of you, or say and do things that devalue or demean you.

Simply wanting approval on the other hand suggests that you would like to have others think well of you and give some sign that you are meeting their expectations. This kind of approval is supportive of self-concept, while *needing* approval generally undermines self-concept.

Try and adopt the attitude that you do not need the self-absorbed coworker's approval to feel competent, worthwhile, or liked. Getting to the point where you can be indifferent to whether or not the destructive narcissist approves of you will go a long way toward being affected by them. If they do approve, very good. If they do not approve, so what? You will not tolerate their trying to take advantage of you, saying or doing things that are demeaning or devaluing, or blaming you. You will have removed yourself from the position of trying to placate them in order to win their approval.

Even if you tend to be somewhat passive and desire harmony, you don't have to seek approval from the destructive narcissist. You can be polite but firm in setting boundaries, acting in a friendly and cordial manner while still not requiring their approval.

Do Not Try to Empathize

You will have to accept that empathizing with the destructive narcissist is futile. You will be putting more and more energy into trying to have a satisfying relationship with this person by trying to understand and empathize with them, only to realize that you are not getting anything in return.

When you empathize with another person you open yourself to their feelings and experiencing. This openness can be somewhat dangerous with destructive narcissists as it gives them access to you and makes it easier for you to accept their projections. Projection occurs when someone gets rid of an uncomfortable or personally unacceptable feeling, puts it on someone else, and then acts as if that person had the feeling. When you accept the feeling, you can identify with it and then act on it. The person projecting the feeling got rid of it, you caught it, and now you have it as *your* feeling. When you accept their projections, you may end up with very unpleasant feelings that you did not have before. And, if you identify with the projection, accepting their perceptions and emotions and adopting them as your own, you may find that you are then acting in accord with it, which is not how you want or intend to act. For example, if you are trying to empathize with a destructive narcissist and they are feeling angry, you may end up feeling angry (you took on their projections of anger), maintaining that anger while the other person feels much better.

A more important reason for accepting that trying to empathize with destructive narcissists is futile is that it cannot make your relationship with them authentically closer or more intimate. You may appreciate it when someone cares enough to try and understand your feelings, and you may feel closer to them because of it. But destructive narcissists do not appreciate these efforts, nor do they feel closer to the person who is trying to understand them. They feel closer to someone who gives them unqualified admiration and is willing to do what they are told to do.

Categories of Destructive Narcissistic Behaviors

Below I've presented examples of behaviors and attitudes of destructive narcissistic coworkers. These categories will help you further in identifying your destructive narcissist and will aid in selecting coping strategies.

Attention

This person:

- always has all the answers;
- speaks loudly, often, and at length;
- interrupts you and others;
- makes "grand" entrances and exits;
- always makes sure to sit at the end of a table for meetings and gets upset if the seats are taken;
- constantly drops names and status;
- almost always turns conversations to self.

Admiration

This person:

- devalues others' work and efforts;

- disparages input from others;
- lacks creativity or originality but trashes or co-ops others' ideas;
- blames and criticizes others to be perceived as superior.

Grandiosity
This person:

- inflates accomplishments;
- is arrogant;
- talks a lot about doing but actually does very little;
- is oversensitive to perceived criticism.

Entitlement
This person:

- gives orders and expects others to obey them;
- expects you to stop what you're doing and attend to them;
- expects to be given preferential treatment;
- does not wait for an invitation to enter your space or sit;
- lies, cheats, distorts, and misleads.

Extensions of Self
This person:

- expects you to do favor, chores, and/or the majority of work on the team, etc.;
- takes credit for work done by others;
- does not knock before entering your space or office;
- uses your possessions without asking.

Shallow Emotions
This person:

- seems to only express anger authentically;
- uses the correct words for emotions, but the feelings do not accompany the words.

Lack of Empathy
This person:

- brushes you or others off when you want to express a concern about their behavior or attitude;

- tells you that you are overreacting if you protest when they blame, criticize, or disparage you;

- will question your needs (being sick, etc.), if they result in an inconvenience to them.

Strategies

Following are some suggestions for actions you can take that may help you better cope with your destructive narcissistic coworkers. These strategies are categorized as active verbal, active nonverbal, passive verbal, and passive nonverbal. As you read through them, reflect on the extent to which you can use a particular strategy. Evaluate the usefulness on the basis of your personality, the work situation, the offense, and possible positive or negative consequences.

Active Verbal Strategies

These strategies require that you verbalize your thoughts and feelings, and this could be difficult for some people. The difficulty arises because of social convention, personal styles, and deep needs to be liked.

- Change the topic.

- Give neutral responses.

- Say, "No," or decline their request.

- Clarify the extent of their or your responsibilities with the boss.

- Firmly, without heat, ask to be treated with respect and courtesy.

- Say, "You're interrupting," and continue talking.

- Tell them you will get back to them. Do not stop what you are doing to attend to them.

- Bring others in the discussion by saying that you want to hear from them.

- Be appreciative of others and praise them instead of agreeing with negative comments about them.

- Ask the destructive narcissist to specify what their contribution will be to accomplishing the task and write it down.

- Point out that they are overreacting, and that this seems to be a habit with them.

- Disagree with the self-absorbed coworker.

- Ask for any orders, directions, etc., they give you to be provided in writing. Do not do anything until you get it in writing.

Advantages and Disadvantages

Active verbal strategies may seem a bit harsh at first. They are not the usual socially acceptable way of interacting with others. However, if you can practice using them with a matter-of-fact tone of voice, you will find that they are very effective and will be so almost immediately. You must be firm when speaking, as inserting qualifiers or being tentative will negate the effect.

There are some disadvantages when trying to use active verbal strategies. You will most likely be uncomfortable, and this will communicate itself to others. Others who do not have the same reaction as you do to the destructive narcissist may consider you as impolite, blunt, etc. Rest assured that, as they work with the destructive narcissist, your reaction will appear less extreme. The destructive narcissist may be puzzled by your change in behavior and start quizzing you about it. The more you use these strategies and increase your comfort level, the more effective they will be.

Active Nonverbal

Although they are termed "active nonverbal," these strategies can also be passive. What makes them active is that you make a conscious decision to implement something that is designed to protect you from the destructive narcissist, something that is out of the ordinary for you. Some may even annoy the person, and you must be emotionally prepared to deal with that annoyance.

- Keep your desk clear and personal possessions locked away.

- Emotionally insulate yourself from their criticism, charges of blame, etc.

- Keep records documenting their behavior, remarks, etc.

- Clearly identify your work, and include your name on all related materials.

- Move away when you see them approaching.

- Cross your arms over chest when they are talking, either to you or to someone else.

- Point your finger at them when you talk. This really annoys most people.

- Show your thumbs. Displaying your thumbs signal dominance, superiority, or even aggression (Pease 1984).

- Drum your fingers when the destructive narcissist is talking. Drumming signals impatience.

Advantages and Disadvantages

Advantages for most of these active nonverbal strategies are that you can take actions that can help you cope, aren't overly obvious, can be easily implemented, and may constitute a minimal approach.

Disadvantages are that you may annoy someone you did not intend to annoy when you use some of the strategies. Some of these strategies seem to be adopting some of the same behaviors that the destructive narcissist displays, like becoming emotionally detached.

Passive Verbal

Passive strategies take the road of least resistance. Implementing these will probably get you a favorable response, but you will have to calculate the price you may pay.

- Agree with whatever the destructive narcissist says.

- Do not challenge misperceptions, lies, etc. Just say something neutral.

- Fawn, compliment, and generally cater to their desire for domination.

Advantages and Disadvantages

Passive verbal strategies are great for keeping the peace. The destructive narcissist will not challenge your agreement with them and will probably consider you as on their "side." The greatest disadvantage is how you may feel about yourself for not standing up for your principles or values. If you value emotional tranquility, you can find passive nonverbal strategies to be helpful.

Passive Nonverbal

Most passive nonverbal strategies preserve harmony, generally at your expense. You may feel that this is the best way to handle the situation. After all, it is not always constructive or helpful to go on the offensive.

- Keep your office doors locked.

- Pile papers, books, etc., on your visitor's chair.

- Avoid the destructive narcissist. Change your schedule so that you do not have casual contact with them. Go out of your way to make sure that you do not have to see or interact with that person.

- Give in to their orders, requests, and demands.

- Lean backward in your seat when talking to them and clasp your hands behind your head. This conveys disinterest and superiority.

- Put your head in your hand when they are speaking. This conveys boredom.

- Rub the back of your neck when they are talking. This conveys "pain in the neck."

- Use the social zone, i.e., more than four feet when you are in their presence. That is, don't stand close to him or her.

- Do not maintain eye contact.

- Wear half glasses and peer over the top at them.

Advantages and Disadvantages

Passive nonverbal strategies put barriers between you and the other person and use delay and withdrawal as avoidance, but can be effective in accomplishing the desired outcome with the destructive narcissist. One advantage is that it is unlikely that this person will be able to pinpoint just what you're doing that keeps you away nor will he or she be able to call you on the tactics. A couple of strategies play into their hands by giving them just what they want. Some, such as those that convey superiority or boredom, will be irritating.

The disadvantages are that you may also distance yourself from other coworkers with whom you could have a satisfying relationship. You may also run the risk of making these gestures and actions routine habits and forget that you are using them for a particular person. You may begin to use them with everyone, including your family. That is not a desired outcome. Stay aware of the nonverbal gestures that can be irritating and make judicious use of them.

It may take a little maneuvering at first, but taking steps to avoid interactions with destructive narcissists will save you considerable distress. You may find that you are already doing some of the suggested nonverbal strategies unconsciously. The other nonverbal gestures may take practice but have the potential for being effective.

Your Behavior and Attitudes

It may be helpful to review your behaviors and attitudes that can and do contribute to your discomfort. Without conscious thought, we all do, think, say, and feel things that play a part in intensifying the discomfort experienced when dealing with the destructive narcissist. Review the following list and see how many of these describe you.

- Talking to the destructive narcissistic coworker, initiate conversations, and/or stop what you are doing to respond to them.

- Failing to emotionally insulate yourself before having a conversation with them.

- Considering this person to be an adult like you.

- Overestimating the self-absorbed coworker's ability or desire to know how you or others are feeling.

- Believing that they would change if they only understood what is distressing in their behavior and attitudes and their impact on you and others.

- Wanting to be polite.

- Feeling afraid of being thought rude by the destructive narcissist.

- Readily accepting your faults when this person points them out.

- Needing to change the person and believing that you can make the difference.

- Wanting to be liked.

- Treating them as you want to be treated.

- Thinking that destructive narcissists do not really mean what they are saying or doing.

- Being willing to give them the benefit of the doubt.
- Not responding to mild forms of your feelings and taking appropriate action at that time. Letting feelings escalate (like not leaving when you become annoyed).
- Observing social conventions.
- Believing that when you make a mistake you are essentially flawed rather than knowing that you can and will do better.
- Isolating yourself from other coworkers.

Social conventions, cultural expectations, past experiences, values, and self-perceptions combine to cause you to tolerate or do things that add to your discomfort.

These are not the only strategies that can be used when trying to cope with destructive narcissistic coworkers. Begin to formulate other strategies that seem consistent with your personality. However, you will also need to become more aware of and work on your attitudes and behaviors that may be encouraging the distressing actions of your coworker. The later chapters provide some guidance for developing your "self" in order to be less affected by self-absorbed coworkers.

Distressing behaviors and attitudes are certainly not limited to coworkers. Bosses can also be self-absorbed. The next two chapters provide information to help you cope with these bosses.

Chapter 4

The Destructive Narcissistic Boss

The boss, like colleagues and subordinates, may also exhibit a destructive narcissistic pattern. It may be even more uncomfortable to work with a destructive narcissistic boss than it is with such coworkers because the boss is the person who evaluates you, determines raises, and decides who gets promoted. Bosses are also able to influence the work environment significantly more than almost anyone else because they are in power positions and have considerable authority.

How can you tell if the boss has a destructive narcissistic pattern? Table 4-1 presents a rating scale for some behaviors and attitudes that are indicative of destructive narcissism when experienced often or almost always. To determine if you are working for a boss who has a destructive narcissistic pattern, complete both sections of the scale in table 4-1. It is important to complete both sections, as you need to have validation of your perceptions.

Table 4-1: Do You Have a Destructive Narcissistic Boss?

Directions: In column I, rate the extent to which you have experienced each of the following interactions with your boss, supervisor, manager, director, etc. In column II, rate the extent to which you have observed the same person behaving that way with others.

5 - Almost always   2 - Seldom
4 - Usually, often   1 - Almost never
3 - Sometimes   0 - Not applicable or unable to observe

	I	II
1. Blames me (others)	1 2 3 4 5	1 2 3 4 5
2. Publicly belittles me (others)	1 2 3 4 5	1 2 3 4 5
3. Makes devaluing comments about me (others)	1 2 3 4 5	1 2 3 4 5
4. Attacks me (others) unexpectedly and often	1 2 3 4 5	1 2 3 4 5
5. Criticizes me (others)	1 2 3 4 5	1 2 3 4 5
6. Gives confusing instructions	1 2 3 4 5	1 2 3 4 5
7. Discourages initiative	1 2 3 4 5	1 2 3 4 5
8. Finds fault, is picky	1 2 3 4 5	1 2 3 4 5
9. Boasts	1 2 3 4 5	1 2 3 4 5
10. Lies	1 2 3 4 5	1 2 3 4 5
11. Makes misleading statements	1 2 3 4 5	1 2 3 4 5
12. Distorts Information	1 2 3 4 5	1 2 3 4 5
13. Inflates accomplishments	1 2 3 4 5	1 2 3 4 5
14. Refuses to admit mistakes	1 2 3 4 5	1 2 3 4 5
15. Does not empathize	1 2 3 4 5	1 2 3 4 5
16. Changes topic to a self-focus	1 2 3 4 5	1 2 3 4 5
17. Takes credit for others work or ideas	1 2 3 4 5	1 2 3 4 5

18. Expects favors	1 2 3 4 5	1 2 3 4 5
19. Expects admiration and/or flattery	1 2 3 4 5	1 2 3 4 5
20. Makes demeaning statements about others	1 2 3 4 5	1 2 3 4 5

Total _____ _____

Scoring

Now, add the ratings for each column. You will want to note if others experience the boss as having the same behaviors or attitudes as you observe. The degree of agreement between the two scores indicates if the way you experience the boss is consistent with the way that he or she acts with others. This allows you to consider if your personal experiences are unique to you or if the boss has a significant number of destructive narcissistic characteristics. If your experience is unique and others see the boss differently, you will want to explore other avenues for understanding what is taking place and how to change it or cope with it. If, on the other hand, it appears that the boss is exhibiting some destructive narcissistic behaviors and attitudes, then the following discussion may be helpful.

Total Score - Column I

80–100   You experience the boss as having considerable destructive narcissistic behaviors.

60–79   You experience the boss as having many destructive narcissistic behaviors.

40–59   You experience the boss as having some behaviors that are indicative of destructive narcissism.

20–39   You seldom experience the boss as having any destructive narcissistic behaviors.

0–19   You never, or almost never experience the boss as having any destructive narcissistic behaviors—Lucky you!

Total Score - Column II versus Column I

80–100   Your observations are almost entirely consistent with your experiences.

60–79   Your observations are generally consistent with your experiences.

40–59   Your observations are somewhat consistent with your expe-
iences but may be subject to distortions by your feelings.

20–39   There is a significant difference between your experiences
and observations.

0–19   Little or no consistency between your experiences and
observations.

What Do the Scores Mean?

When there is consistency between your experiences and your observations, you are very likely to have a boss who has many destructive
narcissistic characteristics. If you have not paid attention to the
boss's behavior and attitudes with others, you will want to become
more observant in order to determine if what you experience is
unique to you or is a consistent pattern of behavior with others on
your level. Examining experiences on your level is important
because the boss may not act this way with anyone they consider
superior in status or of potential benefit.

When what you experience is unique to you and are not vali-
dated by your observations of the boss with others, then there are
other explanations for what is happening. Explanations vary from
person to person and are not the focus for this book. Explanations
include a possible hypersensitivity to perceived criticism, personal
biases or stereotypes, inadequate listening skills, misunderstandings,
etc. While both you and the boss may be contributing to the state of
affairs and this situation may need to be addressed, this book is
focused on destructive narcissism.

Behaviors and Attitudes
on the Scale

Your boss may not exhibit all of the behaviors and attitudes on the
scale all of the time. The level and intensity of characteristics will
vary from person to person. Following are some descriptions and
illustrations for each behavior and attitude.

Blames Me (and Others)

There appears to be a need for some bosses to be perfect, and so
when anything is not perfect, he or she assigns blame to someone
else. Even when what happened is their responsibility, they manage
to find some way to say that you or others are the culprits. They do

not share responsibility for what went awry—others are totally to blame. Further, they are not reluctant to make public blaming statements and to often suggest that those with whom they work are inadequate and are to blame for any mistakes. The blaming behavior is illustrated in the following situation.

The boss of a small department was responsible for developing and presenting a budget for the following year that contained expected expenditures as well as requests for new budget items. The boss had been in that position for several years, so this was not a new task. However, this year the boss forgot to include a standard budget item, one that could be considered elementary. Now, no one else in the department had access to the budget. They did not know how much was allocated to the department, what allocations were designated for different budget categories, how allocations were determined, nor what expenditures were incurred. The only part they played in the budget process was to give the boss a list of new items they wished for the next year. The lists were reviewed by the boss and sometimes their wishes were included in new budget items. But they had no input about or knowledge of standard budget items otherwise.

This year, a particular item that had been requested was placed in the budget, and when the new budget was in effect the item was purchased. Later that year it became evident that funds were not available for that particular item, and adjustments had to be made to cover the unexpected costs by eliminating and reducing some critical standard budget items. This, of course, meant that funds were not available for other promised and expected items that impacted the work of department members. Needless to say, people were wondering what had happened.

The reason given by the boss was that some standard items were not in the budget because of an oversight. The boss assumed no responsibility for the oversight, blaming a department member who was connected in a small way to the overlooked budget item. The boss claimed that this employee should have noticed and made sure it was included. He totally ignored the facts that the employee did not review the budget, had not been asked for any input into developing the budget, and that this was a standard budget item that he, the boss, should have automatically included.

Publicly Belittles Workers

It's belittling when someone makes statements that diminish, lessen, or cut down the other person's activities and accomplishments or that attack the essential self of the other person

Those who belittle may be trying to elevate themselves at the expense of others, may be envious of the other person, or could be just seeking revenge. Most of the time we have no way of knowing the motive.

The destructive narcissistic boss will make belittling comments both to the person's face and behind their back. There are some of these self-absorbed bosses who will not make these comments directly to the person but only to others, then denying that they made the comments if challenged.

If anyone should be bold enough to confront them about their belittling remarks, they will turn it on the other person and accuse them of being overly sensitive and of misunderstanding the statements. They will distort what they said until the other person becomes so confused, frustrated, or angry that he or she is no longer sure of what happened.

Even if the belittling statements are ignored, they can have an impact on how you perceive yourself and how others perceive you. The constant drip of belittling comments erodes self-confidence and positive perceptions and promotes the growth of suspiciousness and self-doubt.

Some examples of belittling statements are:

- "He only got the position (award, etc.) because of connections (race, relatives, etc.)."

- "I do not know why anyone thinks she should be named to the task force. She has not impressed me."

- "Susan, congratulations! I guess you finally got it together and were able to do the job."

- "I do not understand why you can't seem to get this done correctly."

- "You always _____ ."

- "You never _____ ."

Makes Devaluing Comments

Devaluing comments are very similar to belittling comments. The major difference is that belittling usually refers to actions and devaluing refers to the essential character of a person. In this case, the self-absorbed boss devalues who and what the other person is. Behaviors or activities are amenable to changes, the essential self is much less so. Therefore, when devaluing comments are made, they are suggesting that the person is fatally flawed and should be ashamed of being so. Further, the characteristic may be one over which the individual has no control. Included in devaluing comments are those that are racist, sexist, ageist, etc.

Devaluing comments may also be insensitive comments that fail to recognize religious beliefs or that focus on intelligence or physical characteristics and abilities. All such comments are calculated to put down, diminish, or highlight the perceived inferiority of the other person. The intended outcome is to give the impression that the person making the devaluing comment and, by association, their audience do not have these undesirable characteristics and thus are superior. The folks who act as audience for a narcissistic boss such as this would do well to remember that the boss will most likely make devaluing comments about them out of their hearing, naturally considering them inferior.

Examples of devaluing comments are:

- "What can you expect from someone like _____ . After all, he barely got out of high school."

- "Don't expect _____ to be able to do a top-notch job. She has been here for ages and has never really seemed to learn anything. Believe me, getting old hasn't helped."

- "_____ does a better job than you do on this. After all, he did graduate from _____ . You went to _____ , and they are not in the same category."

Launches Unexpected Attacks

The very best bosses do not attack their people. When mistakes are made, misunderstandings occur, or conflicts emerge, the boss with stable or healthy narcissistic development will try to work with the person to correct mistakes and take steps to insure that these mistakes will not happen again. Perhaps clearer communication is facilitated, or conflicts are constructively resolved.

However, when a boss has a destructive narcissistic pattern, they can engage in unexpected attacks on workers. The unexpected nature of these events makes them even more upsetting, as few people, if any, are emotionally and mentally prepared to cope with attacks without warning. After these attacks happen several times, everyone becomes jittery, nervous, suspicious, and more isolated. While you may not be comfortable with unpleasant events, knowing what to expect allows some opportunity to mount emotional and mental defenses that are helpful.

The other important thing to note about unexpected attacks is the unfairness or perceived unfairness. After all, this boss is in the power position and can impact the worker's career, promotion, raise, assignments, etc. Further, the worker is not in a position to respond. So even when the attack is based on accurate perceptions and information, the disparity in status puts the employee at a disadvantage. This relative powerlessness leads to anger, hostility, and frustration.

Do not be confused by the softness of your self-absorbed boss's voice. Just because they're not yelling or do not appear to be angry does not mean that they aren't attacking. This is a mixed message that sometimes does not allow you to realize that you were the brunt of an attack until much later.

On the other hand, you should be careful to be aware of when you may be perceiving something as an attack when none is meant. This misperception can make the situation more complex because you may need to constantly ask yourself if it is a real or a perceived attack.

The following is an example of an attack. You arrive at a meeting and everyone is there, including the boss. When you enter, the boss says, "You're late." Suppose that you are either on time or no more than one or two minutes late. It is obvious that the meeting has not begun, so there is no real reason to call attention to you. If you are substantially later than this, then you know you're late, everyone else knows you were late, and it serves no useful purpose to stop the meeting to tell you something you already know. You have been attacked and put on the spot in order to show that the boss has power.

Is Critical and Never Satisfied

Webster's Dictionary (1999) defines criticism as "the act of criticizing, especially adversally." Therefore, when one is criticized, one's flaws, mistakes, etc., are pointed out with an expectation that these flaws are either fatal or should be corrected

Bosses who often use criticism are apt to defend the practice as one that is intended to help others make fewer mistakes or to become better in some way. However, the definition above points out that the behavior is not meeting that particular objective but is more likely to be punitive and demeaning. Critiquing behavior (making constructive comments) is very different from criticizing someone and has significantly different outcomes.

Being criticized is never pleasant, and it's especially unpleasant when you are unfairly criticized. Unfair criticism occurs when that which is criticized is not under one's control, is a characteristic about which one can do nothing, or is simply not true. Those who are criticized then become defensive, shamed, angry, frustrated, and demoralized.

The critical boss is someone with whom workers seek to avoid interacting for fear of being criticized. It seems that there are very few, if any, interactions with this boss where they are not critical of someone. No one appears able to meet their unrealistic expectations.

An example is when the boss charges you with not providing correct information about something. You may protest that:

- this is not your area of responsibility,

- you were not told that you were supposed to get this information,

- you have no idea to what he or she is referring, or

- you were only passing on the information you were given by others who were supposed to be authorities.

None of this seems to get through as the boss then responds, "You never seem to get it right."

Gives Confusing Instructions

A frustrating behavior of some self-absorbed bosses is their tendency to give confusing instructions. This confusion may stem from their lack of understanding of what they need. That is, they have an idea of what they want, but it's not what they ask for, and then they are upset when you do not read their mind. Or, the confusion may stem from their ignorance. They may not know what is needed and thus ask for the wrong thing. Of course, their error doesn't stop them from being upset with the outcome. Finally, the confusion may result from a deliberate attempt to mislead so that they will appear more competent and you will look much less competent.

Whatever the reason for confusing instructions, those who work with them are generally spinning their wheels and not producing what is needed. Both the boss and the workers then become frustrated.

Once you realize that the boss tends to give confusing instructions you can work to make sure that you better understand what they mean by what they say and what is needed. One way of reducing confusion is to ask for all instructions in writing. If further clarifications are needed, these should also be requested in writing.

Discourages Initiative

Because someone with destructive narcissism can have the attitude and feeling that everything and everyone is under their control, and/or that they must be admired, they will discourage anyone else from exercising any initiative. They must micromanage and dictate what is to be done, how it is to be done, and may become very angry when anyone assumes any initiative.

You will also find them unreceptive to ideas generated by others. The only way to get your ideas accepted is to make the boss think they thought of it or to let them have the credit. However, you may end up very resentful that they are taking credit for your ideas.

It is frustrating to work under these conditions, and when initiatives are discouraged people tend to suppress their feelings, everything stagnates, and the prevailing atmosphere is one of apathy. There is no creativity, enthusiasm, or energy. The lack of interest is evident.

Finding Fault and Being Picky

This characteristic was separated from criticism to highlight an extremely frustrating behavior and attitude. While criticizing is also finding fault, it may not be picky. What I mean by finding fault and being picky is the propensity to find fault with almost everything and to be picky about everything.

The boss who constantly fusses over minor details, who obsesses over irrelevancies, and who expects others to do the same is being picky. It's just not good enough for them that something is done satisfactorily, it must be done *exactly* as he or she wants it done. This attitude leads to resentment on the part of those who have to work and interact with this person, as nothing is ever completely satisfactory.

These bosses may really feel that they have high standards for themselves and for others, but what they have are impossible standards. Neither they nor anyone else will ever be able to realize these ideal standards, and much anguish is aroused by their need for perfection.

Boasts

Boasting is a part of the characteristics of needing to be the center of attention and be admired by everyone. A boss who boasts is sending a clear signal of their expectations that they deserve to be in the limelight and admired.

All bosses should expect a certain amount of fawning and flattery. Some expressions of admiration will be sincere, but many people will say what they think the other person wants to hear, and what they say may not be a truthful reflection of their feelings. Then, too, some bosses do things that are admirable and should be commended. Some work very hard and deserve the recognition of their efforts. I'm not talking about these bosses.

The boss who boasts can expect little in the way of sincere admiration from workers. They will appear to pay attention and to be admiring, but will, in reality, be turned off by the behavior.

Another behavior usually found with someone who boasts constantly is that they tend to ignore the accomplishments of others or try to diminish them in some way. It's as if they build themselves up by tearing others down.

Lies

Lying is very complicated behavior. Usually lies are told to further the person's own ends, like preventing punishment or gaining an advantage. Lies and deceit undermine relationships by promoting mistrust.

Teams and other relationships are dependent on trust between members. Members have to be able to trust each other and this also holds true for the relationship between the boss and workers. When either party cannot be relied on to be dependable, reliable, or to tell the truth, trust cannot be developed or maintained and no cohesiveness will result. Cohesiveness is needed for effectiveness, efficiency, and productivity.

It may take some time before you accept that the boss is lying, regardless of their purpose for the lie. But until you recognize that lying is a characteristic way of behaving, you will be very frustrated and maybe even angry. Most people seem to want to believe the best of others and will make excuses or believe the excuses the boss makes when their lies are revealed. If the boss has destructive narcissism they will also be adept at projecting blame on others. Even when confronted with their lies, these people will continue to maintain that they are blameless and that you are confused or were misled. The end result is that little trust exists between the boss and workers. This mistrust may even extend to team members so that they feel alienated from each other.

Makes Misleading Statements

Sometimes misleading statements are not deliberately made but happen because of inadequate information, misunderstandings, or ignorance. However, what you may find with destructive narcissistic bosses is that they deliberately make misleading statements, such as when they give you part truth and part falsehood. It's hard to

imagine why a boss would want to do this, but having others confused may feed their need to feel superior. If workers act on misleading information, it is also easier for the boss to convince superiors
that the fault is the worker's and not the boss's.

Creates Distortions

It is extremely frustrating to have someone distort what you
said. Most everyone has had an experience where what they meant
was not understood and a distortion occurred. That is exasperating
but is usually easily corrected. However, when someone constantly
distorts what you said, even does so immediately after you say something, it can be almost overwhelming. When there's a difference in
power between the speaker and the receiver such as between a boss
and employee, the sense of helplessness and frustration is increased.

Destructive narcissism can provide a perceptual barrier that
interferes with the ability to accurately hear a message. While everyone filters messages and some distortion occurs, most people are
aware that this could happen and either take pains to reduce the
potential and/or are willing to consider that they missed or misunderstood some part of the message. Those with destructive narcissism do not admit that they could have misunderstood, nor are they
aware of their perceptual distortions.

A boss who distorts what was said is someone with whom it is
very difficult to communicate. At first many who work with a person
like this assume that their own communication skills are inadequate
and try to improve them. However, improving your communication
skills does not reduce the extent to which the destructive narcissistic
boss distorts your statements. You still wind up spending a considerable amount of time clarifying what you said and clearing up the
confusion. Further, being in the power position allows these bosses
to directly or indirectly convey that you were to blame for their
distortions.

Refuses to Admit Mistakes

Some bosses are unable to admit that they made a mistake.
They go to extraordinary lengths to deny any part of an error. It's
always someone else's fault, even when it's painfully clear to almost
everyone that they did make a mistake. It doesn't matter if the mistake is a major one or something of little or no consequence—they
still refuse any suggestion that they made any errors.

A boss who meets this description also manages to have someone else at fault for the mistake. Sometimes they spread the blame

around so that everyone has to shoulder blame at some time, but there are bosses who scapegoat a particular person and this person is constantly blamed for the boss' mistakes. This situation is difficult to overcome, as everyone makes some mistakes and are aware that they do so. By being aware that they can and do make mistakes, they are willing to consider the charge that they made a mistake or had some part in the mistake. When they do reflect on their contribution or admit to any part of the mistake, the boss feels justified in giving them *all* the blame.

Two other outcomes may result: the person is also scapegoated by coworkers and others, and/or, because of the differential in power and status, the person does not have any way of defending against the unfair accusation. The first produces a very unhealthy work environment for everyone because the coworkers have assumed or identified with the boss' assessment of the scapegoated person and are acting as the boss does. Fear, dread, and mistrust become prevalent in that unit, for no one can then be sure that they won't become the next scapegoat.

The second outcome highlights some negative aspects of the power differential. The boss holds all the cards and the worker is helpless to effect a positive change. Their very existence may be on the line as the job is essential for them and/or their family. They are put in a helpless and hopeless position. Staying is miserable but there may be no way out that does not have even more negative consequences.

Does Not Empathize

Bosses that do not empathize can be perceived as cold, aloof, uncaring, and arrogant. It's as if they consider themselves above or different from everyone else. Your feelings are not important to them and they work hard to make sure you do not expect them to understand what you are feeling and experiencing.

They do not appear to care about the impact of their behavior on those who work with them and can be very caustic and cutting in their remarks. If someone tries to make this boss understand their feelings they are doomed to failure, as the boss will change the topic, devalue the feelings, and/or suggest that they are inadequate for feeling this way.

The capacity to empathize is one of the major characteristics of healthy adult narcissism. When bosses have destructive narcissism or underdeveloped narcissism, their capacity to empathize has not been developed and no amount of effort on anyone's part will help them develop this capacity.

The following actual event is an example. A secretary's mother who lived in another state was very ill and she had to take time to go there to make arrangements for her care. While she was there, her mother's condition worsened and she died. The secretary called her boss and told him that she would not be able to return on the designated date because of the death and that she would need to take two to three more days. The boss told her that it was already an inconvenience having her away at that time and that it was inconsiderate of her to ask for additional time. The leave system was such that she could take the time regardless of the boss so it worked out that she was able to stay for the funeral. However, the lack of empathy shown was appalling and permanently damaged the feelings this woman had for her job.

Focuses on Self

The way this plays out is that everything and everyone is perceived in terms of them, even when they seem to acknowledge the existence of others. A cartoon that shows a man talking to a woman at a party illustrates just how this can occur. He says to her, "Enough about me. Let's talk about you. Have you seen my exhibit?" The focus has clearly remained on him.

If you want the attention or approval of this type of boss, everything must be approached in terms of his or her self-focus. They must see that they have a personal stake in what you present before giving any attention. Every conversation, presentation, etc., must concern them and others will receive little in the way of attention or acknowledgment.

An example of this self-focus took place when a department chair told faculty about an illness of one of their colleagues. After noting that the person was ill, the chair shifted the topic to an illness he had several years ago. There was no expression of sympathy for the ill faculty member, just a quick shift to focus on him.

Another example of self-focus is when someone in a unit does something exemplary, like getting an award. While seeming to congratulate the person, the boss really talks about her or his own accomplishments. It's as if the other person existed only to highlight the boss's accomplishments. These bosses cannot allow anyone else to be the focus.

Takes Credit

It is extremely frustrating to work hard on something only to see someone else assume credit for your efforts. It's also true that, when working on a team, the individual's contribution may not receive credit although the team will. That is a different circumstance than when a boss takes credit for an individual's work.

Frustration arises because of the unfairness of the action and because there is little or nothing that can be done about it. If the individual protests, he or she runs the risk of not being believed, of alienating the boss, or of being perceived as uncooperative. The boss is in a position where they are unlikely to be challenged by others, the individual may not be supported by others in the unit, and the differential in power continues to play an important role.

When a boss engages in this behavior the entire unit is affected. Morale is depressed, workers become uncommunicative and suspicious, creativity is negatively impacted, and productivity suffers. Those in the unit are reluctant to advance ideas, propose solutions, or work cooperatively as they fear that they will not receive credit for what they do. The atmosphere becomes one of cautiousness, playing it safe, and making sure that one is covered.

Expects Favors

Some bosses expect workers to perform personal favors for them and/or to give them gifts while getting nothing in return. Generally, most people are willing to do favors and some do not expect anything in return. However, some do expect some reciprocity in the relationship; when they ask a favor of you they expect you to repay them in kind. Even if you do not necessarily expect anything in return and are pleased to do favors for others you may have reservations about being *expected* to do favors for someone. It's probably their air of entitlement that is very offensive. Further, this sort of boss will expect favors without their having to ask for them. In other words, people who work for them are expected to volunteer to do favors and to do so frequently.

Few bosses will openly demand that their birthdays be recognized, but if the boss is a destructive narcissist then he or she will expect workers to remember their birthdays and to provide presents. The same is true for other holidays where presents could be given. There is no open acknowledgment that this is an expectation, but it does not take long for most people to get the message.

Loves Admiration and Flattery

Many people are able to tolerate a small amount of flattery, especially sincere flattery. It's pleasing to hear that someone thinks highly of you or of your accomplishments. Insincere flattery can fool you some of the time, but most people begin to recognize when flattery isn't really meant.

Bosses who constantly seek admiration and flattery do not appear to care if it's sincere or insincere just as long as you continue to tell them they are wonderful. After all, this is how they perceive themselves and they think it only fitting that you mirror their perception. They assume that the flattery is only a true statement about them and wouldn't think to question its veracity.

Again, there is an unspoken expectation that others will provide the flattery and anyone who does not do so is thought to be jealous, bitter, uncooperative, or insensitive. The boss may even consider you to be self-centered if you're not willing to give them this admiration and flattery.

When someone seeks to be honest and authentic it is very difficult, if not impossible, for them to engage in insincere flattery. They try very hard to mean whatever they say and expect others to do the same. This situation can make for considerable conflict with a boss who is looking for admiration and flattery.

Others may take a more practical approach and consider that if this is what the boss expects, then go ahead and give it. They assume the attitude that it does not matter in the long run if they provide insincere flattery if it makes for smoother relationships with the boss.

Demeans Others

It is difficult to know what to say when a boss makes a demeaning statement about someone to you. Are you expected to agree? Or are you free to disagree, since you may have another opinion? Further, if the boss is making these kind of statements to you about someone, are they making demeaning statements about you to others?

This boss is engaging in behavior that is designed to build him- or herself up at the expense of someone else, to find out what your opinion of the other person is, or to make sure that everyone stays somewhat isolated from others at work. Whatever the reason, you still have to make a quick decision about your response.

If the boss is building him or herself up at the expense of others, then you will find that no one is quite up to their standards and they probably *are* making the same kind of statements about you to others. If he or she is trying to find out what your opinion is, then they will probably report it to the person, distort it in some way to them, or tell the other person that you have this opinion but that they do not. Either way you wind up as the "bad guy," and the boss has managed to divide colleagues.

It may be to the boss's advantage to have workers remain somewhat isolated as that reduces the risk that the boss will face a challenge about some of their negative and destructive behaviors and attitudes. Each individual remains convinced that they are the only ones that feel this way or are experiencing the boss in this way. Each one then becomes less confident and more doubting of their self-efficacy while their self-esteem suffers, bitterness emerges, jealousy and envy are prevalent, and productivity and morale suffer.

All of the behavior I've outlined in this chapter can make working for your self-absorbed boss an unpleasant and tricky proposition at best. The next chapter will provide you with a variety of coping strategies to help you negotiate the minefield more easily.

Chapter 5

Coping with the Destructive Narcissistic Boss

Chapter 4 described some behaviors and attitudes that categorize the destructive narcissistic boss. This chapter describes some suggested strategies that you can adapt for your particular situation to help you maintain a cordial working relationship while also preserving your emotional equilibrium. Underlying assumptions in this section on work relationships are:

- that you need or desire to develop effective working relationships,
- that these relationships do not require you to make too many sacrifices to maintain,
- that the strategy does not insist that you buy in to the triggered feelings or cause you to act in opposition to your values.

The Strategies

As you work through the list of suggested strategies, try to visualize yourself and your particular situation and think about how these strategies can be used or adapted to allow you to make reasonable accommodations.

Table 5-1 presents potential coping strategies for each destructive narcissistic behavior. You always have the option to seek other assignments or other employment. However, it may not be in your best interest to do so. The coping strategies presented here assume that you remain in your present situation. The potential coping strategies that are listed are categorized as active or passive. I use "active" in the sense that you have to put forth some effort to take action that is designed to promote a viable working relationship with the destructive narcissistic boss and to also maintain a sense of personal integrity. "Passive" is used to denote strategies that will preserve harmony with the boss or that are withdrawal or avoidance strategies. Both have their uses and strengths as well as possible weaknesses. Your personality, self-esteem, and personal situation all play a part in deciding which strategy will be most effective for you. Each strategy is briefly described.

Table 5-1: Potential Coping Strategies

Strategy	Category
1. Do not confront	Passive
2. Seek other assignments/employment	Passive
3. Verify statements	Active
4. Use constructive listening and responding	Active
5. Choose noncommittal responses	Passive
6. Attend to their expectations	Passive
7. Get it in writing	Active
8. Keep records and documentation	Active
9. Do not take it personally—detach, use emotional insulation	Active
10. Ignore fault-finding	Passive
11. Make self-affirming statements	Active
12. Understand the constraints or parameters—let initiative go	Passive
13. Do not resort to sarcasm	Active

14. Do not bitch, moan, complain	Active
15. Do not go over their head—except as part of a group	Active
16. Change your expectations	Active
17. Avoid, ignore	Passive

Do Not Confront (Passive)

Confrontation is an invitation to the other person to examine their behavior and its impact on you. The key words here are "invitation" and the "impact on you."

Destructive narcissists will not accept any invitation to engage in self-examination. They do not see any need to review what they are doing or saying, as they consider that they have a perfect right to do and say whatever they please. Nor do they note or care about the impact of their behavior and attitudes on others. They cannot see that what they are doing has a negative impact and are more inclined to consider this to be the other person's problem. Confrontation does not work because they neither see nor care. All too often confrontation is perceived as an attack, that you're telling someone off or trying to knock them down a peg—all very negative and usually destructive reasons to confront. Confrontation for these reasons is not usually very effective either.

Some, or even many, people in power positions do not like to be confronted. When the characteristic of destructive narcissism is added to needs for status and power, the rejection of confrontation by that person is even more intense. It does not matter if you are an expert at constructive confrontation. Destructive narcissistic bosses will not be receptive to any suggestion that they examine their behavior and its impact, no matter how tactfully you may present it. Further, they are most likely convinced that they do not make mistakes. Because they tend to blame others, they will manage to turn it back on you so that you will wind up even more confused, angry, frustrated, and despairing. Save your efforts for more productive strategies.

Also remember that they are in a power position and that their opinions of you will make a difference in your work environment, raises, promotions, etc. If you attempt a confrontation and they are not receptive, you may be in a worse position than when you started.

It's difficult for most of us to understand that someone with destructive narcissism is not able to accept others' perceptions of their behavior and to take an objective look at what they are doing. Most people, even if they do not agree with the other person's perception, will be willing to look at their behavior before rejecting the other person's point. They will try to work out the conflict and maybe even compromise. Those with destructive narcissism do not see any need to examine their behavior nor to compromise. This is another reason why confrontation is unlikely to be effective.

Seek Other Assignments or Employment (Passive)

One possibility is to go somewhere else, to another unit, another job, or even another state. Sometimes the situation is so distressing that this appears to be the only option. Moving is certainly preferable to continuing to work under circumstances like those I've outlined, especially when it appears that the destructive narcissistic boss is in their position for some time to come.

It may be helpful to consider this as the last option if there are not other compelling reasons for moving. That is, try some of the other strategies first, keeping in mind that you can fall back on this strategy. By making this *an* option, not *the* option, you do not rush into a hasty decision, allowing yourself to make a carefully considered and researched decision.

For some, moving may not be a viable option. If they move they may not be able to find an equal position elsewhere that has the same benefits, satisfaction, salary, etc. Moving may not be the best thing for a family because:

- the other spouse may have an established career,
- the children may be at a point in their schooling where moving would be disruptive,
- they may have elderly parents for whom they have major responsibilities,
- family members may have health problems, and on and on.

There are many reasons why individuals do not or cannot use this option.

Verify Statements (Active)

It may be helpful to adopt an attitude and practice of verifying statements. It is not that you do not believe what others tell you—it's more a need to make sure that you understand not only what was said, but also what was meant.

It is not unusual for people to get things mixed up or to misunderstand something, particularly if the communication is oral rather than written. The personal communication filters that all of us have contribute to misunderstandings and distortions.

When you work with a destructive narcissistic boss you may need to adopt a mind-set that whatever they tell you needs to be verified in some way. You will need to exercise some discretion and not be openly skeptical and questioning, learning more subtle ways for making sure that you have the correct information.

For example, suppose the boss tells you that you violated a particular policy. Rather than assume that you did violate a policy, look in the policy manual and see if there is such a policy, or check in some other way. You may find that there is no such policy and therefore you could not have violated it. You still may not be sure what game the boss is playing, but you will have two pieces of information: no such policy exists, and you are not in violation.

Use Constructive Listening and Responding (Active)

Constructive listening and responding involves hearing both the content and the feelings expressed in what the other person is saying, and making your responses direct. It sounds simple but can be very difficult to do.

The primary part of every message is the feeling component. Content is also important but can be misleading if feelings are ignored. You do not have to directly respond to feelings, but they should be taken into account when you formulate your response.

For example, if the boss blames you for a mistake, the content of the statement is pretty evident. The boss's feelings may not be as evident but, in some ways, may be more important. The feeling accompanying the blame may be a sense of satisfaction that their perception of you as flawed is confirmed, that their feeling of superiority is reinforced, or that you are not under their control. The identified feeling along with the blaming comment helps you make a more constructive response.

For example, if the feeling is one of satisfaction, the response could be one that acknowledges the mistake and notes that it is helpful that someone like the boss is there to find the mistakes before they are disseminated. If the feeling is one of superiority, the response could be a noncommittal one that does not accept responsibility for the mistake. If the feeling is that they need more control, the response could be one that says you will send everything to them in the future to check before it is sent out.

To increase your skills in listening and responding, try to get in the habit of paraphrasing before making a response. When you paraphrase what someone says you restate what you thought you heard. This gives the other person the opportunity to correct any mistakes in what they said or in what you thought you heard. Your response is more apt to be on target if you paraphrase first.

Another tactic is to focus on the feelings and to respond to them before responding to content. For example, in the instance described above, if you were to respond to feelings you could note that mistakes really seem to anger or irritate the boss or that it is very important that no one who works with them make mistakes. By focusing on feelings, you emphasize what the sender considers important.

Choose Noncommittal Responses (Passive)

These responses are intended to neither agree nor disagree, to neither indicate right or wrong nor what is good or bad. These responses are neutral and indicate only that the other person has been heard.

These neutral responses:

- can prevent distortions of what you said,

- will not give the other person ammunition with which to attack you or to carry to others, and

- allow you to preserve your sense of integrity.

When working with a destructive narcissistic boss, you will find it to your advantage to become as neutral as possible. This state of neutrality will help if you want to preserve a cordial working relationship, prevent attacks, and prevent your comments from being distorted and passed on to others.

Generalized responses such as "It can be difficult," "I understand what you mean," and "You don't have an easy job" can be appropriate for many different situations. For example, if the boss is talking to you about one of your colleagues and is making very demeaning statements about them, you don't have to either agree or disagree with the statements. You can say something like, "Humans are very complex, aren't they?"

Attend to Their Expectations (Passive)

One sure way of maintaining a cordial working relationship with a destructive narcissistic boss is to attend to their expectations.

Be attentive, flatter them, and do favors. Try to anticipate what they want and be the first to provide it.

For example, if the boss wants to be the center of attention, then you can make sure you mention their accomplishments publicly whenever possible. You can see to it that they receive credit for most all of the work done by attributing the product to their leadership and organizational skills. There is usually some measure of truth in doing so, and this small nugget is what can be emphasized.

If the boss expects recognition, you can make sure you nominate him or her for some honors. This can be risky, as some people get more upset at not winning than they would if they had not been nominated. Other forms of recognition are organizing their office birthday party, giving them gifts, and providing social events such as lunch or dinner.

If you choose to attend to their expectations you must be aware and remember that you will not receive anything in return. You will not be able to rely on any good will on their part or expect any favors in return. Some may make an effort to let you know that you are meeting their expectations, but most will accept your attentions as their just rewards. These bosses feel they are entitled to have their expectations met without any effort on their part and that you are only doing what you are supposed to do.

Get It in Writing (Active)

You will save yourself much frustration and agony by getting requests, directions, directives, etc., in writing. If you have ever experienced the frustration of doing what you understood or were told to do, only to have the boss then reject it and blame or criticize you for not getting it right, then you understand the value of making sure that you receive correct instructions before beginning a task.

A destructive narcissistic boss will do things such as telling you to do something and later denying they told you to do it while heaping criticism on you for having the gaul to attempt such a thing. Other examples that highlight the value of getting it in writing are:

- The boss gives you a due date that turns out to be incorrect.

- The boss tells you to do a report or other time-consuming project, and when you ask for directions and guidelines they tell you there are none and for you to use your best judgment. When you complete the project or report they tell you it is incorrect because you did not complete it according to the guidelines.

- The boss gives you an assignment and later asks you why you're working on it, as it's not your responsibility.

- The boss tells you what he or she will be using for evaluation of work performance for raises and then uses different criteria.

- The boss says they will support you for a promotion but later cannot recall doing so.

Another situation where getting it in writing is helpful is after meetings, either one-on-one or with a group. You will find it useful to draft a memorandum immediately after a meeting that presents your understanding of what transpired, especially decisions and promises that concern or impact you. For example, if in a meeting the boss asks you to take on an additional assignment and promises resources to help and the reward you can expect, your memorandum would present your understanding of the scope of the assignment, the promised resources, and the reward.

When there are group meetings where the boss is present, suggest that someone take minutes that will then be distributed to attendees for corrections. The minutes can also serve as a record of what was decided and the designated responsibilities. This will prevent much confusion, many misunderstandings, and considerable frustration. Everyone will be informed, and it can reduce the number of side deals that are made as there is a record of what was agreed to by the group.

In short, get in the habit of communicating more in writing. While it may cost time and paper to do so, you will find that it actually saves time and reduces emotional wear and tear in the long run.

Keep Records and Documentation (Active)

Along with getting directions, assignments, understandings, etc., in writing is the need to keep records and documentation. It can be helpful to have a paper trail or to be able to substantiate your efforts, and you never know when you may need to do so when you work for a destructive narcissistic boss. Further, if it becomes known that keeping records is a habit of yours, when you say you did not receive some notification, you are likely to be believed. This will help prevent the boss from saying that he or she sent you a directive when they didn't.

Keeping records and documentation requires some organization on your part, as you also need to be able to retrieve the information when needed. Some records may be as simple as making notes on a calendar or keeping a weekly list. Other people may need a file folder to keep paper copies of notes, memos, etc. It may also be help-ful to keep copies of e-mail that involve instructions, promises, or anything that may be called into question at a later date.

This may sound very time consuming but, with a little thought, keeping records and documentation can be easily and quickly accomplished. It does not take much time to make notes after a meet-ing, or to jot a note on an appointment calendar after a meeting or phone call. Take notes during a meeting and put them with all other materials in a folder correctly labeled. It could also help your per-sonal organization if you took ten to fifteen minutes at the end of a day or week to write a list of accomplishments, assignments, etc. Doing so not only provides a record but can increase your awareness of your productivity.

It is regrettable that keeping records and documentation will have to be a part of your work environment. But it's better to put forth the effort than to be taken aback or flustered at your inability to support your claims or to correct misperceptions, misunderstand-ings, and lies.

Do Not Take it Personally (Active)

Destructive narcissistic bosses will make insensitive comments intentionally and unintentionally. They also make demeaning, blam-ing, and criticizing comments that will trigger feelings of rage, anger, frustration, inadequacy, incompetence, unworthiness, and so on. There is little you can do to prevent them from making these com-ments and, while there are techniques and strategies you can take to prevent these unpleasant feelings from being triggered, these tech-niques and strategies must be learned and practiced to be effective. One strategy that you can use almost immediately is to emotionally detach—that is, do not take the destructive narcissistic boss's com-ments as personally directed at you even when they may seem to be. If you can ever reach the point where you react to their comments with calming, rational thoughts like: "That's their opinion and while they are entitled to it, that does not mean their opinion is correct," you will reduce or eliminate many of the unpleasant feelings you experience. You may not care for their comments, but you do not have to buy into them, believe them, or end up feeling bad about yourself because of them.

It's wonderfully freeing to realize and accept that you do not have to react negatively to these comments. While you may never reach the point where you will have no reactions, by letting these comments roll off you like water off a duck's back, you can reduce your discomfort.

A deep understanding of why the unpleasant feelings are triggered is the best strategy, but that takes guidance and a commitment to deep introspection, learning new ways of behaving and reacting, and considerable practice. It can be done and is very beneficial to your personal growth and development. I encourage you to embark on this journey, but it's beyond the scope of this book.

If, on the other hand, you want to protect yourself until you learn new behaviors and reactions, emotional insulation is useful. By using emotional insulation, you put a barrier between your feelings and the triggering comments.

Exercise 5-1: Your Emotional Insulation

Materials: A sheet of paper, crayons or felt markers.

Directions: Visualize a wall, a shade, a fence, a gulf of some sort, or anything that provides a barrier between you and the destructive narcissistic boss. Once you have your barrier visualized, draw it to fix it in your mind more firmly.

Visualize the barrier as preventing the triggering comments from reaching your feelings and put the barrier in place before all interactions with this person. Focus on your imaginary barrier during the interactions. Think about how it looks—its length, breadth, width, color, material, etc. Fortify it to keep it strong and protecting. With some practice you will be able to use it effectively whenever you need it.

You may find that you can use your emotional insulation the best when you are prepared in advance for an interaction, such as a meeting. You may find that you are less prepared for impromptu interactions and that these are causing you distress because you do not think to engage your emotional insulation. The more you practice engaging your insulation, the more you will be able to call it up when needed.

Ignore Fault-Finding (Passive)

Sometimes the best strategy is to ignore your boss's negative behavior, and fault-finding is a great place to start. You will have to accept that you cannot meet their every need, want, or expectation, and no matter how hard you try these bosses will always find something that does not meet their standards. They appear to go out of their way to find something wrong.

Have you ever had the experience of trying to please an "unpleasable" person? You worked hard to make sure everything was done to the best of your ability, including remembering what they liked and trying to correct or prevent anything they did not like. You were focused on getting it as perfect as you possibly could, and were probably pleased at how well it turned out. However, when you presented your efforts to the person, they were complimentary but pointed out where it was not perfect. What they noted was mostly likely a minor flaw or one that was of no consequence, but they still took the attitude that your effort was nice but not what they had in mind. It was then hard for you to remain pleased about all your good work because that person was able to find fault with it. It did not much matter that 98 or 99 percent was excellent—the minor part that was not to their expectation ruined the whole thing. Possibly you became frustrated, angry, felt inadequate, wondered if you could ever please them, and had other unpleasant reactions.

When working with someone like this there are numerous opportunities for them to find fault or be picky. If this happens frequently then workers understandably become frustrated and angry. Some may redouble their efforts to please, but even they realize after a while that they are not making any headway. Some may give up or exact revenge in unacceptable ways, such as hostility.

If you want to simply avoid continuing to experience the unpleasant feelings, you may wish to just ignore the fault-finding and focus more on the positives in the situation. If the flaws or mistakes in your work are of little consequence, they too can be ignored or corrected in the future. We all strive to improve our work and can use the input that helps us to do so.

Make Self-Affirming Statements (Active)

Many attitudes and behaviors of destructive narcissistic bosses produce self-doubt, guilt, shame, and diminished self-confidence, self-esteem, and self-efficacy. Affected workers may begin to question their abilities and competencies even when there is considerable objective evidence that they are indeed competent, able, efficient, and productive. If, or when, you find yourself in this position, an effective strategy is to use positive of self-talk, such as making self-affirming statements.

Self-affirming statements focus on your strengths and highlight them instead of focusing on your flaws and magnifying them to produce guilt and shame. They are statements about you that can either be made silently to reinforce your self-esteem or voiced out loud to present an alternate perspective. Further, do not forget that embedded in each weakness, fault, or flaw is a strength. These strengths can be enhanced and built on rather than continuing to try to remediate what someone else considers to be a weakness, fault, or flaw.

It works best to use one of two kinds of self-affirming statements: the first highlights your strengths, and the second focuses on a strength hidden or embedded in a weakness, fault, or flaw. Highlighting your strengths reminds you that the blaming, criticizing, and demeaning attitudes and behaviors of the destructive narcissistic boss do not define you, that you are considerably more than that. Identify specific strengths and competencies that are crucial to your job performance. Skills and strengths such as your attention to detail, your ability to organize the work, define the problem, or work at something until you get it right, your ability to type fast and accurately, or whatever is important for your job. Then when a blaming, criticizing, or demeaning statement is made to or about you, say your strength either to yourself or aloud. Say it aloud when appropriate, such as during the following situation.

The boss criticizes you for not getting something in at a particular time. It may or may not have been due at that time, but the boss is berating you about not submitting it on time and some very bad feelings are welling up inside you. It can be very helpful to you if, instead of explaining or making excuses to your boss, suppressing anger and hostility toward them, or allowing yourself to feel incompetent, shameful, guilty, etc., to focus instead on your strengths. You could respond, "I took pains to make sure the job turned out right. I do attend to details." It is self-affirming to realize that evidence of a strength can be embedded in a perceived fault, weakness, or criticism. To identify some personal strengths try the following exercise.

Exercise 5-2: Affirmations List

Make a list of frequent criticisms of yourself that you and/or others make. You do not have to agree that the criticisms of others are correct to list them. After making the list, consider each of them separately and see if you can identify one or more strengths that the criticism somehow highlights. These can then be used as the basis for self-affirming statements. A few examples of criticism and embedded strengths follow.

Criticism	Possible Strengths
Speaks loudly	I can be heard. I seldom have to repeat statements.
Procrastinates	I want to get all possible data and think it through before acting. I value gathering others' input.
Impulsive	I'm spontaneous, creative, and open to new experiences.

Understand Constraints, and Parameters (Passive)

Destructive narcissistic bosses are not apt to tolerate others' initiatives. Indeed, they are more likely to micromanage and to stamp out any signs of creativity or initiative. They are not creative and mistrust or refuse to recognize others' creativity. They also fear that things will not be under their control if they allow others to exercise any initiative. These fears drive them and their behaviors and attitudes.

It may be difficult for you to accept that your initiative is discouraged and no matter what the potential benefits may be, the boss will dump cold water on the idea. If you are a "take charge" kind of person and want to move ahead on what you consider to be an appropriate initiative, you will not only run into considerable opposition, you will irritate and alienate the boss. Accepting the constraints or parameters of what is expected and allowed is one effective strategy to defuse the situation.

You may have the fantasy that you can change the boss so that he or she will see the merit of your ideas. Be aware that this notion simply reflects your need and is a fantasy. Even if the boss will hear you out, they are unlikely to change their mind. If they appear to agree that you can move ahead, they will then find some means to undermine your initiative and efforts so that you do not succeed. It's far too optimistic to think that you can change this person to meet your needs. Understanding that discouraging initiatives provides some measure of safety and security for the boss is a part of accepting the constraints and parameters under which you work.

Do Not Resort to Sarcasm (Active)

This strategy is considered active because you have to make a conscious effort to not be sarcastic. Many people who are frequently sarcastic have to remind themselves to not make these remarks. You may get some satisfaction from using sarcasm as an indirect way of letting the boss know how you feel, but in the long run it can be ineffective and damaging to you and your relationship with the boss. Your frustration and anger do not concern the boss, and he or she is unlikely to be affected by your feelings one little bit. Your feelings are of little consequence in their world and letting them know what you are feeling is simply irritating to them.

Some people resort to sarcasm because it is indirect and they aren't comfortable directly expressing their feelings. Sarcasm allows them to express these feelings (usually unpleasant ones) and can be used to try and devalue the other person. Sarcasm is also used to demean, put the other person in their place, and to tell the other person off, as well as helping the sarcastic speaker feel superior. All in all, there appear to be no good, constructive reasons for using sarcasm.

You may be tempted to resort to sarcasm after trying more direct ways of communicating your feelings, ideas, and thoughts to the boss only to have them rejected, devalued, criticized, or ignored. You may have tried confronting them, but that did not work either. The ensuing frustration may lead you to consider using sarcasm. You would do well to reconsider, as the outcomes will probably be more damaging to you and to your career.

The destructive narcissistic boss may be hypersensitive to perceived criticism. This hypersensitivity makes them see blame and criticism where none was intended, and they are hyperalert to anything that seems to them to be less than total admiration. It is for these reasons that they are unlikely to miss sarcastic remarks or let them slide. Their antennae are finely tuned, and they pick up even a hint of sarcasm. Do not underestimate this hypersensitivity.

Do Not Bitch, Moan, or Complain (Active)

Another strategy where you have to be conscious and mindful not to do something is described in the following discussion. By taking mindful steps, you are being active. One way of venting is to express your frustration, anger, etc., openly. When this frustration is expressed in terms of what the other person, such as a boss, is doing, saying, or meaning, it is commonly termed bitching, moaning, and complaining. When your frustration is openly expressed without a target or the suggestion that the other person is to blame, then you are accepting responsibility for your feelings. In other words, you admit that you are frustrated, not that someone "caused" you to be frustrated.

This, of course, does not mean that the other person did not do something to trigger the frustration—they probably did do something, and if you work with a destructive narcissistic boss, you will experience considerable frustration. Even so, the feelings are still yours. You have the power not to be frustrated regardless of the provocation, and you can consciously choose not to let these uncomfortable feelings be triggered.

Venting your feelings, especially in the workplace, does not resolve the feelings nor solve the problem. All it does is to add to the general atmosphere of lowered morale and dissatisfaction. Further, you run a risk of having your comments carried back to the boss and used against you. Venting can be somewhat helpful if done with a trusted coworker or outside the workplace with someone you trust.

Venting to destructive narcissistic bosses is definitely a no-no. These bosses are not in touch with their feelings, do not care about others' feelings, and fear intense emotions and any expression of them. These are some of the reasons you will find venting to the boss to be counterproductive. Your hope, when you vent, is that the other person will care enough to take needed action to reduce or eliminate the situation causing your uncomfortable feelings, such as frustration or anger. You hope that you are important enough to him or her to care about your feelings and be willing to work to resolve whatever produced the feelings. No one who can be characterized as a destructive narcissist has this level of caring for others, and the destructive narcissistic boss has power in addition to their indifference to others.

You will find it beneficial to your workplace relationships to restrict or eliminate bitching, moaning, and complaining. Engaging in these venting behaviors is not likely to result in constructive changes. Confine your venting to a trusted few.

Go to the Boss's Boss (Active)

This is only an effective strategy when the entire unit agrees to present their concerns as a group to the boss's boss or supervisor. The individual or group that goes over the boss's head is more likely to be perceived as malcontent and dissident and can find their situation worsened.

There are several reasons why the destructive narcissistic boss's negative behaviors and attitude are not seen or are ignored by their boss. You need to remember that the relationship, behaviors, and attitudes of your self-absorbed boss with *their* boss are very different than they are with you. For example, destructive narcissistic bosses admire status and power and want to be perceived as similar to those in power, so they mirror many of their behaviors and attitudes, especially when they are with the person who has status and power. Think about it—how do you feel when you interact with someone who is very much like you? You are charmed and feel this is a person you like and admire. This is what happens very often between the destructive narcissistic boss and his or her boss. You and the boss's boss will have very different perceptions based on different experiences.

Some destructive narcissistic bosses may mirror their boss's self-perception. That is, they reflect back to the boss how they see themselves, not necessarily objective reality. Just think of it and put yourself in the person's place. Here is someone who relates to you as you perceive yourself to be. How refreshing it is to know there is someone who sees you as you see yourself and likes what they see. No wonder the boss's boss is not receptive of criticism of this person.

If you decide that *something* must be done and feel that those in charge *need* to know what the destructive narcissistic boss is doing, take that step only if you have the support of your coworkers. Support in this instance means that some or all of your coworkers physically go with you to the boss's boss and/or sign the complaint letter. This is one time you do not need to be out front and alone.

Change Your Expectations (Active)

You have certain expectations of yourself and of others. These expectations are found on both the conscious and unconscious level and play roles in your reactions and triggered feelings. Expectations of others are also influenced by what their roles and relationships to you are. These expectations are formed by prior experiences, learning, and interpretations of events. They form a perception of what you want or expect the boss to be and do.

Sometimes these expectations will be adjusted to be more in line with objective reality, reacting to how the boss really behaves and acts, but these adjustments tend to be relatively minor. For example, you may have an expectation that a boss will insist that everyone be at their station at 8 A.M. However, at your new workplace the boss institutes some modified flex time and only insists that the job be done. He or she is not insistent that everyone be in place at a certain time. Or, you may work in a job where it is expected that you call on customers before coming into the office or sometimes must stay late, and therefore you can sometimes arrive later than others. These are relatively minor adjustments and are usually easily accomplished.

However, the adjustments needed when you work for destructive narcissistic bosses are not minor. They need careful consideration and may mean making a conscious decision to change on your part. You may also struggle with having to perceive and accept your boss in a way that is at odds with your characteristic way of relating, and this can make you very uncomfortable. For example, it is difficult for me to accept that another person cannot empathize with someone on some occasions. I don't expect anyone to empathize with most everyone, or to empathize most of the time, just to be able to empathize with someone some of the time. By extension, I often believe that if this person can empathize with someone that means he or she has the ability to empathize with me. Having to accept that a person *cannot* empathize is completely foreign to me and extremely difficult.

When working with destructive narcissistic bosses you may have to accept and adjust to several of the characteristics listed in table 5-1. When you accept the boss as they are, you change your expectations of their behavior, attitudes, and ways of relating. You also save yourself much mental anguish.

Avoid and Ignore (Passive)

Two passive strategies for dealing with a destructive narcissistic boss are to avoid and/or ignore them as much as possible without putting your job in jeopardy. You may wish to reflect on how often you do initiate contact with the boss, how often this contact is critical, and how often you are caught by him or her for impromptu interactions that leave you upset, confused, frustrated, etc. Both of these situations provide opportunities for reducing interactions with the boss that are not threats to your job security. Reducing these interactions can reduce the times you experience the uncomfortable feelings and increase your sense of self-efficacy.

As you reflect on how often you initiate contact with the boss, you will also want to explore your motives for doing so. Are you asking indirectly for reassurance from them? Are you fulfilling a need to have the boss perceive you as similar or as different from everyone else? Do you really need data, answers, or information directly from the boss, or are there other ways of obtaining it? Do you need a favor? Why do you initiate this contact? There are times when you have no alternative but to initiate contact, but you will want to have it clear in your mind that there aren't other alternatives. When you have no other alternative than to initiate contact with the boss, put your emotional insulation firmly in place and do what is needed.

If some of your interactions are initiated by the destructive narcissistic boss and tend to be impromptu, you can initiate some avoidance strategies to reduce these occasions. Examples of impromptu interactions are:

- you walk into the main office to pick up a report and they see you and call you into their office, or

- you meet in the corridor, and they stop you to talk.

Developing strategies that fit your circumstance takes a little thought but can have a significant payoff in terms of reducing interactions that leave you upset.

Ignoring some things can help you cope, but this is more easily said than done. You want to be circumspect and judicious in what you choose to ignore. You cannot afford to ignore everything. A guideline that may help is to ignore everything that does not directly have an impact on your job. For example, if the destructive narcissistic boss blames you for something, and you and everyone else knows that it was not your fault, you could ignore it. Or, if the boss brags about an accomplishment, you can ignore it. Another example is when the boss demeans or devalues someone else. You do not have to respond—you can ignore what was said and change the topic.

You may be in the habit of attending to the other person when you're involved in a conversation. Using eye contact, a slight forward lean, listening intently, and screening out distractions is considered polite behavior by most. Attending may be second nature to you and ignoring someone very difficult. But it will be to your benefit to go against your training and try it. You will have to decide to ignore the boss at times and practice doing so before you can realize these benefits. This is an instance where you may have to protect yourself by behaving at odds with what you want to do or with what you feel comfortable doing.

Summary

Dealing constructively with destructive narcissistic bosses is not an easy task, but it can be done and done in a way that does not demean you or jeopardize your job. The most difficult thing to accept is that you cannot change the boss or cause them to modify their behavior. If you reflect on interactions with them that were most upsetting, many were upsetting partly because you tried to get them to change and they did not. For example, you tried to explain where they had their facts or assumptions in error with the expectation that if they knew what was correct they would no longer blame you. It was probably very upsetting to realize that:

- nothing you said made any difference,

- they continued to blame you to the point where they shifted the focus of the blame to your failing to make sure they knew these facts long ago, even when they already had the information,

- you had no way of knowing they did not know the facts, or

- it was not your responsibility.

What was probably most upsetting was that you were unable to effect any change in the boss's behavior or attitude.

Since the option of change is out for them, you will have to rely on other strategies, especially if you are not in the position where you can leave. The seventeen strategies presented in this chapter give you some suggestions with which to work. These will probably trigger additional ones that fit you and your situation. The underlying basis for all the suggested strategies is that you want to preserve a working relationship that does not cause you stress and mental anguish.

Chapter 6

The Boss's Perspective

It is usually more difficult for the boss to identify destructive narcissistic workers than it is for workers to identify a destructive narcissistic boss or coworker. The difficulty has many causes, among which are:

- the destructive narcissistic worker is similar to the boss in many behaviors and attitudes,

- many destructive behaviors and attitudes are ignored or explained away by the boss,

- this worker behaves differently with and toward the boss, and

- the boss reacts positively to the charm and flattery of the destructive narcissistic worker and refuses to listen to any suggestions that this person is disruptive.

Bosses' personal underdeveloped narcissism may also play a role in their inability to see the impact of the destructive narcissistic worker.

Similarities

Many self-absorbed people do quite well in their careers, whatever they are. They manage to convince others of their worth and tend to get promoted and to be able to find jobs. These people can be charming and manipulative, and these two qualities can be helpful in getting ahead. Or perhaps both the boss and the worker can have many characteristics in common, and neither considers the characteristics as liabilities. For these and other reasons, the boss sometimes does not perceive the havoc wrought by a destructive narcissistic worker.

For example, if a destructive narcissistic worker tends to be adept at blaming others and refuses to admit making mistakes, their boss may mirror the same behavior. This is the boss who can always find something or someone to blame for errors, etc. This boss feels at the mercy of inferior people and that they have to tolerate people who constantly make mistakes, cause delays, give wrong information, and are generally incompetent. This boss feels, and usually says, that if it were not for him or her, nothing would ever get done, or done correctly, and that any errors were caused by others. Is it any wonder that they either do not see this characteristic in the destructive narcissist, or don't understand it? They may even consider it to be admirable. After all, the boss is seeing a reflection of him- or herself in the other person and likes what they see. Most everyone tends to admire others that mirror a part of self they consider positive.

Ignore Irrelevancies

A good boss needs to know when to ignore irrelevancies. Some things are not worth the time and effort it would take to respond. Positive characteristics of effective bosses are the ability to stay focused on the task at hand, and to emphasize goals, productivity, efficiency, and outcomes. Further, trying to deal with "people" problems can be frustrating and unproductive, with many bosses feeling uncomfortable when confronted with the intense emotions of workers.

These can be some of the reasons why bosses will ignore or explain away distressing behaviors and attitudes brought to their attention. They simply do not want to get involved in trying to deal with some behaviors that, on the surface, may not appear to them to be disruptive or serious. They ignore the fact that someone else finds these behaviors distressing and that they may signal something deeper and more serious.

The person reporting the distressing behavior may also find it difficult to explain why what the other person did was so upsetting and, if the boss has not experienced the person in that way, the boss may feel that what was done was misunderstood or that the reporter is overreacting. For example, can you adequately explain that you feel threatened, violated, and disrespected because your destructive narcissistic coworker puts his name on reports and never gives you and others who work on these reports any credit? You are the one who can wind up looking petty and complaining if the boss does not consider this to be important. Further, if you use the intense feeling words above to describe your reactions, the boss may think you are just overreacting. You may be overreacting to this particular event, but all too often the overreaction occurs because it's just one more in a series of unacknowledged and unaddressed events. However, you cannot or do not explain all of this, and so the boss can conclude that you are making a mountain out of a molehill. Trying to explain to someone who is removed from the experience with the destructive narcissist is difficult.

It can complicate matters when you wait until you are fed up or overwhelmed before going to the boss about the coworker and, as a consequence, have intense feelings that are very evident. Bosses do not like to have to deal with others' intense emotions. Intense emotions are messy and do not contribute to productivity. Therefore, the boss's first reaction is to lessen the intensity of your emotions, and unfortunately, most bosses respond by trying to be logical and objective. This can easily leave you feeling misunderstood and discounted. There are at least two reasons why your feelings are being misunderstood or discounted. The first reason is the one described above that is unintended. The second reason can be that responding this way is how the boss manipulates others. This can be especially true if they are too a destructive narcissist. The destructive narcissistic boss ignores or explains away what the coworker did and focuses on lessening the intensity of your feelings. Either way, it does not take long to realize that the boss is not going to be responsive about your concerns.

Different Behavior

The destructive narcissistic worker is very likely to behave differently with the boss than with coworkers. Therefore, bosses will not understand what about the described behaviors and attitudes are distressing as this is not their experience of that person.

For example, the destructive narcissist will blame, criticize, and belittle others to their face but are most unlikely to criticize or belittle the boss. All the boss ever hears from this person is praise and flattery. This coworker may intentionally mislead or lie to you but is careful not to do so with the boss. If it turns out that the information they provide is wrong, this person is quick to say that they were only repeating what someone else said, and may even label you as the source.

The boss then is faced with conflicting perceptions. One perception is that this person acts in ways that are frustrating and anger provoking to their coworkers. The other perception is of a pleasant, charming person who the boss has never observed doing any of the things described and who has been pegged by the boss to be an adequate or exemplary worker. The boss can begin to wonder if this person is being misjudged, picked on, or scapegoated by colleagues, especially if the destructive narcissist mirrors some of the boss's characteristics.

Charm and Flattery

Charm and flattery, also known as "sucking up" in some cases, are useful to practice if you want to get ahead. Most everyone reacts positively to people who seem to like, admire, and praise them. It's almost impossible to disagree with or feel negative about someone who seems to like you and is very open about it. They may even think you are wonderful, and it is very uplifting to have someone feel this strongly about you. It could also be that their feelings about you are confirmations of how you feel about yourself.

It can also be difficult to differentiate between sincere and insincere flattery. If you adopt the attitude that all flattery is insincere, then you miss an opportunity to connect with someone who values you in a positive way. You may even unintentionally make them feel stupid for trying to let you know how they feel about you. While you can develop a knack for detecting insincerity, it does take time to develop, and even then you still have no way of knowing when you are wrong until it is too late. This is another reason why a boss may be susceptible to flattery from the destructive narcissist.

Then, too, if the boss has some grandiosity, a sense of entitlement, feelings of being unique and special, and/or a need for admiration, the charm and flattery of the destructive narcissist finds fertile ground and flourishes. After all, the boss's personal opinion is being mirrored by the destructive narcissistic worker. It's hard, if not impossible, to disagree with someone who has the same admiration for you as you hold for yourself. In this case, flatterers are more likely to be perceived as astute persons who are good to have around because they "see you clearly." It can be very demoralizing and scary when the boss and a colleague are both destructive narcissists.

Identifying the Destructive Narcissistic Worker

How does a boss go about identifying a destructive narcissistic worker? Why would they want to identify this person? What can they do even if they do identify them? These are but a few of the questions that this section and chapter address.

There are numerous reasons why it is to the boss's advantage to determine if there is a destructive narcissistic worker in the unit. These reasons include team building and morale, productivity, managing conflict, and keeping valuable employees. The destructive narcissist can have a negative effect on everything and everyone in the unit. Some of these effects are discussed later in this chapter and developed more extensively in chapter 8, "Effects of the Destructive Narcissist on the Unit or Team."

If you're a boss trying to discern why you or others on your team have such trouble with a particular employee, you can use table 6-1 to determine whether you're dealing with a destructive narcissist. Using the form as a means of identification is particularly useful if you, as the boss, have received complaints or expressions of concern about a worker from many of their coworkers, but you do not experience or perceive them in this way.

Finally, I've provided several suggestions about coping strategies. After identifying the destructive narcissistic worker, the boss can take steps to lessen the impact of their behavior and attitudes on productivity, creativity, and other workers in the group. The suggestions presented are general and should be reviewed with your particular situation and goals kept in mind. These are not intended to be "one size fits all" but can be triggers for creative and constructive solutions that are appropriate for your work setting.

Table 6-1: Behaviors and Attitudes Suggestive of a Destructive Narcissistic Worker

Directions: Following are some behaviors and attitudes that, when clustered, suggest a worker with destructive narcissistic characteristics. If you are rating more than one coworker, rate each person separately using the indicated scale. Use a combination of your observations (for instance, "Demonstrates little or no creativity" and "Often does favors for you") and consistent reports by coworkers (like "Makes misleading statements" and "Finds ways to off-load work onto others").

5 – Almost always	2 – Seldom
4 – Frequently	1 – Almost never or never
3 – Sometimes	0 – Not applicable

1. Belittles others *condecends*
2. Devalues others' work and accomplishments
3. Feels superior to coworkers
4. Makes unflattering comparisons between coworkers

5. Is quick to praise and flatter you
6. Tries to be seen with you often
7. Begins to dress, talk, walk, etc., like you
8. Joins your clubs or social groups
9. Makes sure they share your interests
10. Often does favors for you
11. Appears inordinately proud of self
12. Is never at fault for anything
13. Makes blaming and criticizing comments about coworkers
14. Makes misleading statements
15. Is arrogant or cocky
16. Finds ways to off-load work onto others
17. Appears insensitive to the impact of their behavior
18. Does not display emotions other than anger
19. Tries to get you to flatter and approve of him or her
20. Demonstrates little or no creativity
21. Does not have a sense of humor
22. Makes sarcastic and cutting remarks to coworkers
23. Staff, or others in a subordinate position, are intimidated or report feelings of intimidation
24. Coworkers and others report being attacked by this person
25. Inflates tasks, contributions, and/or accomplishments

Add your ratings. Scores that fall between 85–100 indicate that you are dealing with someone who has a considerable number of destructive narcissistic characteristics; scores between 70–85 indicate someone with many of these characteristics; scores between 55–69 indicate someone with a lesser number of these characteristics; scores between 40–54 indicate someone with few of these characteristics, and scores below 40 indicate almost none of these characteristics. Pay particular attention to items rated 3 and above.

What the Scale Items Mean

Below I've explained a little bit more about how certain behaviors and attitudes of a destructive narcissistic employee might affect you and the group you oversee. Read along and see how familiar these items sound.

Belittles Others

You may need to listen carefully for belittling statements made by this person because they can casually drop them into a series of seemingly innocuous statements. You may discover that these belittling comments can be consciously overlooked or not recognized as belittling, but on some level are able to influence your opinions. I call these kinds of statements "poison pellets." They poison your perception without you really realizing it, especially if you get numerous such statements over time. This person never says anything that can be openly challenged, just little snippets that most people will let go by. An example of a poison pellet statement is when someone says that a coworker does good work when they can be counted on not to be sick.

Destructive narcissists tend to be envious of others and consider themselves as the only ones who are really unique and special. They may have fantasies of unlimited power, success, wealth, beauty, etc., and feel that others are inferior to them. In order to maintain their sense and stance of superiority, they must denigrate others and do so by belittling them and their accomplishments. They seek to elevate themselves and their accomplishments at the expense of others.

You may feel that you are not influenced by these belittling comments and are able to be more objective, and that may be true. However, it's also likely that you are influenced on a level below conscious awareness by the destructive narcissist's belittling comments. Many people like to think that they form their own opinions of others, but most everyone is influenced in ways that are subtle and indirect. The whole field of advertising uses this concept very effectively.

Devalues Others

In addition to belittling, destructive narcissists may also devalue others' work or accomplishments. The impressions they try to give is that the other person did not really do or accomplish much, that they were able to achieve only because of some special treatment they received (like affirmative action), or that they are taking unearned credit for the work or accomplishment. They try to show that much ado is being made about very little.

This behavior can be especially corrosive to a positive perception of the person as the devaluing statement may contain a grain of truth. For example, the person being devalued may be a minority and the firm is supportive of affirmative action. However, that has nothing to do with that person's accomplishments or quality of work. The positive perception can be eroded with the unmentioned, nagging suspicion that this person is being favored in some way because he or she is a minority, and you may not be consciously aware of how this suggestion is working on you.

Feels Superior

Destructive narcissists often have deep feelings of superiority arising from grandiosity, an inflated self-perception. These feelings in turn also support their feelings of entitlement and of needing to be considered unique and special. As adults, they have learned how to mask these attitudes and feelings so that they are not readily apparent to others and it may take considerable time before this attitude is recognized.

These are the people who constantly promote themselves at the expense of others, engage in name-dropping, and make belittling and disparaging comments about others. Both elevation of self and denigration of others are used to bolster these feelings of superiority. For example, this person may take every opportunity to insert into a conversation the names of those they consider as having higher status. Usually the names are also paired with them in some way so that they can bask in the reflected glory.

They boast, brag, and keep their names and self constantly before you, as you are the boss. They make sure that you have every opportunity to consider them as a cut above everyone else by boosting their accomplishments and downplaying everyone else's. It may be wise to maintain some skepticism about the person who is constantly telling you how wonderful they are and how much they do, especially when these feats are presented in comparison to everyone else.

It is not easy to judge when someone has feelings of superiority, as this is an internal state where the person may either be somewhat unaware of the feelings or deny to self and others that these feelings exist. The feelings of superiority can be inferred from their behavior, especially what they say about themselves and about others. There are even times when the masking is so good that others perceive them as having an impoverished self-concept—that they are promoting themselves and undercutting others in an attempt to feel better about their "self." The reaction to an impoverished self-concept is very different than that for feelings of superiority.

Makes Unflattering Comparisons

Another behavior that is suggestive of destructive narcissism is making constant unflattering comparisons between coworkers. The destructive narcissist's comments may seem to cast one coworker in a more favorable light than the other, but closer examination will usually reveal that both are being denigrated.

The focus for this characteristic is on the constant nature of the behavior. No coworker is ever good enough or performs as well as they do. It's not so much that they criticize a coworker for not meeting some unspecified standard, as it would be very unusual for everyone to be fully able or competent all of the time. It is their tendency to almost always make unflattering comparisons.

The comparisons can be about almost anything—work, personality, physical characteristics, personal habits, education, family, etc. There is a subtle inference that these people are, in some way, not quite adequate. Because they focus on coworkers and are not comparing someone with them, they reduce the risk that they will be seen as self-boosting.

Praises and Flatters

It's very pleasing when others recognize your accomplishments and find them praiseworthy. A large part of our self-confidence and self-esteem development comes from how others treat and perceive us, and letting us know of their approval through praise is a very direct way to communicate. Praise for a job well done or for accomplishing a difficult task can be motivating.

Praise needs to be differentiated from flattery. "Flattery" is defined in *Random House Webster's College Dictionary* as "excessive or insincere praise" (1999, 499). The intent of flattery appears to be to try to manipulate a person through praise that is insincere. However, when sincere praise is used with the intent of currying favor, promoting oneself, and gaining approval, the praise then becomes flattery. Praise is "the act of expressing approval or admiration; strong commendation" (1999, 1035). That definition implies that the approval is given with no hidden agenda or motive.

In their efforts to sustain their feelings of superiority and be perceived favorably by those in power, destructive narcissists will be quick to praise and flatter those perceived to be powerful or of higher status. The destructive narcissist may not even know if they are being sincere. However, receivers should be alert to the possibility that the expressions of admiration and approval sent their way will have a hidden agenda, and they are receiving these expressions because of their position, not because of their person.

It's probably not worth the time and effort to try to distinguish the sincerity of praise from the insincerity of flattery. You will do yourself a disservice if you assume all expressions of approval and admiration are insincere and have hidden motives. After all, you are probably deserving of some, if not all, of it and would not want to reject it or the person. However, if there is a person who constantly expresses admiration and approval, especially at every opportunity in a public forum, you may need to entertain the idea that this is flattery designed to win your approval and advance that person.

It is easy to be mislead by flattery because most people would like to think well of themselves and having someone else affirm a good opinion of self is satisfying. Also because many people are reluctant to think or believe that others are deliberately being insincere. Some are even like sponges, soaking up every little bit of praise and flattery to bolster a sagging self-concept. Destructive narcissists use all of these reasons to their benefit to manipulate and can be very successful at it. You may not realize what happened until the destructive narcissist starts being critical and drops you because you are no longer useful. Their admiration and approval are given to the next person perceived to be powerful and helpful to their advancement.

Wants to Be Seen with You

In addition to name-dropping, destructive narcissists try to be seen with you, the boss, as much as possible. They bask in the reflected power and status of the boss's position and feel that they are somehow gaining by gaining proximity. After all, they must be superior to others because they get to associate with the boss.

Being seen chatting with the boss, going to lunch, and attending both work-related and social events are all vigorously sought. If the boss is the kind of person who considers personally attentive workers as expected and necessary, this person is just what they want and need. The boss likes the attention and the destructive narcissist is eager to provide it.

On the other hand, if the boss is not particularly needful of this attention they can still play into the destructive narcissist's agenda by being unmindful what that person is doing. This boss simply does not see what's taking place and how they are being used to further the aims and ambitions of the destructive narcissist.

Books and other writings on how to be successful point out the importance of being perceived as similar to those in power and suggest adopting some of their more surface and obvious characteristics, such as dress. The unconscious mechanism of identification can be triggered to the extent that subordinates begin to identify with the boss and adopt many of their mannerisms. All such identifications are not destructive narcissism. It becomes so when many of the other described characteristics are also present.

Destructive narcissistic workers will almost always take on the more identifiable traits of those perceived to be in power positions. They will dress, talk, and walk in similar ways to the point where they want to shop at the same stores, buy the same brands, use similar speech patterns and tonal inflections, and adopt many of the nonverbal body positions. For example, I once observed a woman dean who changed her hair style to be the same as that of the woman provost. They may not be aware that they are doing this, and as the process of imitation takes place over time, many around them are also unaware of what's taking place.

This imitation is also one of the reasons why a boss may not recognize the destructive narcissist; after all, the boss is looking at an image or reflection that mimics their characteristics, of which they approve and accept. It's usually quite difficult to critically examine yourself, and as many bosses simply don't even try, the destructive narcissistic worker remains unidentified.

Remember to try to understand this behavior in context with other behaviors. The person who imitates the boss may be doing so in order to "fit in" and become a group member. Imitation may also be an unconscious act, as many nonverbal behaviors are not fully in the person's awareness. The person may genuinely admire the boss and simply want to be more like them. There are many reasons why the boss may be imitated and not all of them are reflective of destructive narcissism. This is why it is important to look at a cluster of behaviors and attitudes plus personal reactions to the person over a period of time.

Joins Your Clubs and Social Groups

Social interactions can be a road to receiving favors, promotions, increased earnings, and other positive outcomes for a career. People let down their defenses and allow others to get closer and more intimate in more social situations. These are some reasons why the boss's clubs and social groups are sought-after activities for some workers. Playing on the same softball team, belonging to the same church, and pursuing other social and club memberships that the boss belongs to are examples of how workers seek to become more like the boss and to become better positioned for receiving preferential treatment. The assumption is that it is much harder to criticize or chastise someone with whom you socialize on a frequent and regular basis and it is easier to give these people preferential treatment. This assumption appears to be born out in many different settings from the lowest to the highest. The old saying, "It's not what you know but *who* you know" has a lot of truth to it.

Destructive narcissists will use this tactic to the point where they will make a complete changeover in order to be close to the boss. The changeover may not occur all at once, but often occurs gradually, over a period of time. Many bosses will not recognize what is happening and some may even welcome the attention and flattery implied. This "social climbing" too is a behavior that is part of a cluster or pattern and should not be looked at in isolation.

There are careers where the social and professional are expected to overlap and interact, such as corporate management, law, sales, etc. There are also company-sponsored recreational team sports where workers play together regardless of position and status. These are situations where the destructive narcissist does not have to make any effort to socialize with the boss but may also be in competition with others. In this situation, the destructive narcissist will generally also seek additional sources for social interaction with the boss so as to be considered unique and special.

Tries to Share Your Interests

Most everyone is drawn to those who share their interests, whether it be golf, psychotherapy, spiritual issues, art, jazz, or stamp collecting. This is one reason why there are so many professional, social, and hobby-related clubs and organizations. People like to associate with those who have similar interests.

When people are introduced to each other they generally take some time to find out what interests they may have in common beyond the obvious one of being in the same place at that time. Even when they know there are commonalties, such as both are accountants, they still try to find other commonalties and shared interests. This is one way that colleagues and acquaintances become friends.

Destructive narcissists will make sure the interests of the boss are ferreted out and adopted. This is done to further that person's aims and ambitions, not because the interests are genuine. They only appear to share common interests but are probably a lot less interested than they appear. Because the motives for their behavior are internal and hidden, other people cannot know what they are and are easily misled.

There is another possible reason for a destructive narcissist to make an effort to share interests of the boss—that is to try and fill the emptiness within by engaging in activities that others who are perceived as having power and status seem to find pleasurable. Activities are one way to keep from staying in touch with uncomfortable emotions and to ward off despair and depression. While some people find satisfaction in activities, the destructive narcissist neither gains satisfaction nor pleasure.

Does Favors

Without consciously realizing what is taking place, some bosses fall into an expectation and behavior that can prove to be unwise, that of having workers do favors for them. Destructive narcissists will be eager to curry approval from the boss by doing favors to the point where the boss may come to rely on them.

An outcome for the expectation and behavior can be the unrealistic expectations of the person doing favors that they, in turn, will have favors done for them, be considered superior of their colleagues, and receive unearned rewards. The impact on other workers can be a feeling that the boss is playing favorites. This perception can really hurt morale.

This state of affairs can be particularly troubling if the boss is prone to asking for favors of a personal nature. Asking for personal favors can imply a personal relationship beyond what actually exists, and some people are quick to capitalize on the misperception. Another way that this behavior can be troubling is when the boss's requests for favors comes across to workers as an order or as an entitlement.

Favors of a professional nature can also have pitfalls. When the boss asks for a professional favor, workers can mistake this request as singling them out as being special. Destructive narcissists in particular will take this as a signal that they are considered by the boss to be superior, unique, and special, and they will begin to find ways to capitalize on their position of being "in" with the boss. If a boss is not careful, the destructive narcissist can engender considerable disruptiveness in the unit's morale by making deceptive and misleading comments attributed to the boss that this person says they heard because of their special relationship with the boss.

Displays Inordinate Pride

Inordinate pride is exemplified when people exaggerate their accomplishments and self-worth. It is not so much that they simply have high self-esteem as that they think they are vastly superior to almost or everyone else. They also tend to be overly proud about personal conditions and situations over which they had no input or control, such as their ancestors, family wealth, beauty, intelligence, etc. It's not a usual sense of pride that is referred to here, but an overblown and sometimes unwarranted sense of pride. The prevailing attitude of these people is that who they are and what they do rate self-admiration and admiration from others. They seem to make sure at every instance that their perceived superior status or characteristic is kept in the forefront.

Being able to feel pride and pleasure in one's self and at one's accomplishments contributes to healthy and high self-esteem. These feelings promote self-confidence as well, and, as such, this sense of pride is desirable. It's possible to be proud of who you are, your family and ancestors, privileges, personal characteristics, etc., without going overboard by assuming that these make you superior to others and that you should be recognized and admired for them. It becomes a matter of attitude that then influences behavior.

The destructive narcissist seems to walk around and interact with others with the attitude of the wizard in the Wizard of Oz who termed himself, "I am the Great I Am." They boast, strut, pose, sneer, and generally try to make sure that everyone knows their self-perceived superior status. They also tend to be drawn to those who give them the admiration they seek and tend to denigrate those who do not appear to be sufficiently admiring.

Bestows Blame and Criticism

The destructive narcissist is adept at blaming and criticizing others and can do so when seeming to be making positive comments. Even in the most benign-seeming statement about another, there almost always seems to be a denigrating statement or criticism embedded. If challenged, disagreed with, or asked to explain, these people will say that they were misunderstood, that they said something else, or will waffle in some way if they feel the boss may disapprove.

They may also make these comments in a provocative way to elicit agreement and obtain additional comments from the boss. For example, the comment that "_____ is always angry" can be intended to gain confirmation that the boss, too, experiences the person as angry. They hope to gain an additional comment from the boss that he or she does not approve of the person, or that the boss lacks confidence in the person's ability to function, or that the person is being closely observed. By gaining these additional comments, the destructive narcissist bolsters a personal sense of superiority through blaming and criticizing others.

The destructive narcissist can be quick to blame and criticize others but is also adept and quick to take credit where little or none is due.

Needs to Appear Blameless

Some people find it difficult to admit making mistakes and errors, even to themselves. Yes, something went wrong and they realize it and may even accept their responsibility, but they are very reluctant to openly admit it. No one really enjoys admitting mistakes and errors, but many feel that this is one way to assume responsibility and demonstrate maturity, so they will admit making a mistake in the hope and conviction that it can be corrected and will not happen again.

Destructive narcissists, on the other hand, do not consider taking personal responsibility for their mistakes and errors. They will find ways to say or suggest that they are not at fault because others misled them, did not do what they were supposed to do, or are deliberately trying to make them look bad. Sorting out the real state of affairs can be difficult, especially in a very competitive environment where coworkers may indeed engage in these behaviors to gain an advantage. Since you cannot know if they are sincere because this is an internal state known only to the individual, it is too complicated to try and find out what really happened, and so the destructive narcissist is seldom challenged and can continue to shirk personal responsibility for mistakes and errors.

Here's a good example of not accepting responsibility. A destructive narcissist does not get something in on the due date, but instead of accepting personal responsibility or requesting an extension because they did not do what was needed, they say that it's someone else's fault that it was not completed on time. These people rationalize that someone else *must* be to blame because they are never at fault for anything.

Even when they start to say something complimentary it usually ends up with a criticizing tone, implication, or comment. For example, a destructive narcissist may remark, "John always dresses well. How can he have so much money for clothes on his salary?" Or "Suzie finally got the report in. I bet she got Ray and Bill to do most of the work." No one is ever good enough to meet their standards. If challenged about the critical part of their comment, they will maintain that they were being complimentary and that you misunderstood. Their attitude is one of, "How could you ever think I could be faulted?"

Makes Misleading Statements

It can be easy to miscommunicate without any intention of doing so. Even people who know each other very well can mislead and misunderstand on occasion, and it happens frequently among people who have to work together and do not know each other well. The English language lends itself to these kinds of miscommunications, where the same word can have different meanings so that what is being said and meant is not what is heard and understood, although both are using the same words.

Destructive narcissists are prone to intentionally making misleading statements. They do this in many ways—by using an official's name as the originator of information so as to make what they say more authoritative and believable, by misquoting you and others, by drawing unwarranted inferences, and by withholding information. Again, if challenged in any way, they deny any responsibility for the misleading statement and usually assert that they were misunderstood.

Because we all know how easy it is to unintentionally misspeak and thereby mislead we tend to overlook and excuse others when they do so, perhaps feeling that it was unintentional and they did not mean to mislead us. Most people tend to be somewhat forgiving of mistakes. However, when a person constantly makes misleading statements about matters that should be known or could be easily verified by that person, then it increases the possibility that this person is making deliberate attempts to mislead. It's interesting to note that this person will seldom make misleading statements to the boss. However, they frequently make misleading statements to coworkers and then deny having done so.

Displays Arrogance

A sense of entitlement and grandiosity contribute to arrogance and cockiness, which are displayed in both verbal and nonverbal behaviors. Both entitlement and grandiosity are internal states that cannot be directly observed by others but can be inferred from comments and behaviors observed over time. Indeed, the arrogant person may not even be consciously aware of displaying these attitudes.

Some nonverbal displays of arrogance and cockiness include the following body positions and gestures.

- A significant backward lean while looking at others from under lowered eyelids, giving an impression of "looking down their nose" at others

- A facial expression of distaste, dislike, etc., paired with a backward lean
- Sitting at the head of the table when not in charge of the meeting
- Entering someone's office or workplace without knocking or waiting for an invitation, especially with coworkers

Some verbal and combinations of verbal and nonverbal behaviors that indicate arrogance and cockiness include the following.

- Interrupting a conversation or a speaker
- Making demeaning and disparaging comments about coworkers
- An inflated sense of self-importance exhibited by boasting and bragging
- Demands that their needs or wants be taken care of before others'
- Self-aggrandizing comments
- Sarcastic responses to coworkers' suggestions and input
- Finding something negative about almost everything coworkers propose
- Giving orders to coworkers without authority to do so

Off-Loads Work

The following example illustrates how a destructive narcissist can off-load work onto well-meaning coworkers who want to be helpful. John was on a trip and had taken his wife along. His wife had a chronic medical condition but was cleared by the doctor to take the trip. However, she fell ill on the trip and had to be hospitalized, and when John called the office, the doctor termed her condition as grave. He had appointments set up with important customers when he was to return from the trip but was not sure he would be able to keep them and, because of the importance of the customers, asked the boss to try and get coworkers to cover for him. This was easy to accomplish and all of his coworkers agreed to cover these appointments even though, for some, it meant considerable shuffling of their schedules and other commitments.

After all of this, John and his wife returned on the date they'd originally planned, and she resumed her usual schedule. He came back to work but refused to take back the work coworkers had agreed to do. The coworkers were now in a position where they could not back out. John managed to convince the boss that it would not be proper for him to reassume these appointments and that he was still too shaken at his wife's illness to do so. Note that his wife was in the hospital and that was not a deception, but it is unlikely that the condition was as "grave" as it had been portrayed. Needless to say, John's coworkers were furious at his behavior and felt angry that their cooperation was exploited and that the boss was fooled by John.

This is a somewhat extreme example of off-loading work, but I have seen it happen. Sometimes a more senior coworker who has this tendency to off-load work will simply give it to a junior coworker. The more junior person may not feel secure enough to refuse to do it or may have the mistaken notion that any senior person can give them work. The boss remains unaware of the exploitation, and it can continue for some time. There are many other ways to off-load work, and destructive narcissists can usually to bully or exploit their way into some free time by getting others to do some of their work.

Insensitive

Destructive narcissists seem insensitive to the impact of their behavior on others. The word "seem" is probably not accurate, and it could be that the word "is" is more appropriate. At any rate, the behavior and attitude ends up being the same.

These self-absorbed people are taken aback when someone challenges then protests about how they are being treated. The narcissist's attitude is one of disbelief that they could be so misunderstood and that the other person is being unreasonable or is emotionally disturbed. For example, destructive narcissists will consider it perfectly acceptable to call a coworker a liar but cannot understand why that person would become angry. Their response would then be to term the person emotionally disturbed because he or she became angry. Destructive narcissists' feel entitled to say whatever they choose to and expect the other person to accept it. It's understandable that the self-absorbed person sees the world this way considering that they consider themselves infallible and ultimately superior.

This is also the kind of person who feels that coworkers are overreacting when:

- they expect credit for work done in collaborative projects and become angry when the narcissist grabs it all,

- coworkers are appalled or critical of them boasting, bragging, and constantly engaging in other self-promotion, and

- coworkers ask for courtesy and respect and set firm, clear boundaries.

The destructive narcissist does not seem to understand and appreciate others as separate, worthwhile individuals.

This insensitivity extends to making comments that ignore cultural, racial, gender, and other differences or conditions, such as illnesses or disabilities. The depressed person is told to "get a grip," the racially different person is referred to as "you people," the person with a different religion is told that their religion is a "cult" because it is not mainstream, a woman is told that she should not let her PMS interfere with work when there is no evidence that she has PMS, and on and on. These kinds of comments will be made, and when people protest or object, they are told that they are too sensitive, that they misunderstood, or are asked if they are emotionally disturbed. The self-absorbed response indicates a total lack of understanding of the impact of this behavior on others.

Lacks Emotionality

It may be refreshing to a boss to have a worker who does not display intense emotions, as these displays can be uncomfortable for both parties. This may be one reason why the boss tends not to recognize destructive narcissists. However, what the lack of emotionality may be masking is that this person has a shallow range of emotional expression, except for anger.

Most adults with healthy narcissism have a considerable range and depth of emotions that are felt and can be displayed. Most can also control these emotions, and many know how to make sure that they are exhibited under appropriate conditions, although there may be occasions where the feelings are so intense that they break through the control. Destructive narcissists not only experience a limited range of emotions, but the depth and intensity of their emotions are also extremely shallow. These conditions apply to all their emotions except for anger, which, like that of the infant, can be overwhelming, consuming, intense, and difficult to control. Indeed, their anger is more akin to rage and fury, which is scary to them and to others.

While this person does not experience the uncomfortable feelings that most others do, they also do not experience the more positive emotions such as happiness, joy, contentment, satisfaction, pleasure, etc. They may laugh but do not really understand humor (a characteristic of healthy adult narcissism), may express appropriate feelings without actually experiencing them, and continually wonder what it is that others seem to feel that they do not.

Solicits Flattery and Approval

Everyone appreciates approval and praise but some people actively solicit these. The manner of solicitation may be indirect, but these people appear to have a constant need for admiration and approval, especially from the boss and others considered to be in power. An inordinate need for flattery and approval is seen in the following behaviors and attitudes.

- Fishing for compliments and statements of recognition

- Trying to be a superman or superwoman

- Feeling dissatisfied with having less than the biggest or best

- Flaunting or showing off possessions

- Spending money to impress others

- Overspending or going in debt to obtain unneeded material things or services

- Bragging

This is not an exhaustive list, but it provides some examples of behaviors that are easily observed and, when combined with other characteristics, indicate destructive narcissism. Wanting to be admired and have others' approval are not destructive traits, but when they become excessive and constant, they do indicate that there is under-developed and possible destructive narcissism.

Exhibits Little or No Creativity

Creativity is also a characteristic of healthy adult narcissism. Creativity is not limited to the artistic realm but is inclusive of originality, novelty, and inventiveness in all aspects of life. New ideas, processes, and products are also evidence of creativity and indicate a freedom of thought to explore new ways of being and doing.

Destructive narcissists, by definition, do not have healthy adult narcissism and so are not creative. Any new ideas that they propose have been stolen from others. Left to their own devices, they cannot come up with an original thought but are quick to capitalize on the creativity of others. Even when it appears that they've produced an original or creative product, such as a paper or book, further examination will reveal that some other person did most or all of the work or that the whole product was stolen.

It can be difficult for a boss to discern a lack of creativity on the part of a particular worker, but listening well and noting the absence of anything original can provide clues. Listening to other workers also provides clues as to the originator of ideas.

Has No Sense of Humor

As noted before, another characteristic of healthy adult narcissism is a sense of humor. A sense of humor is the ability to be amused at life, at oneself, at events. Being able to laugh at oneself indicates that you are able to understand that you are not perfect and accept these imperfections, and that you take yourself seriously but not *too* seriously.

Destructive narcissists are not able to step back from "self" and be amused at imperfections. They are not able to see the absurdities in events, life's ironies, and other activities that give people a chuckle.

Humor has great physical and psychological benefits. It highlights ironies and incongruities, encourages flexibility and adaptability, and aids in making connections with others as noted by Hafen, Karren, Frandsen, and Smith in their book, *Mind/Body Health* (1996). So, there are many and good reasons for cultivating a sense of humor.

Destructive narcissists evidence a lack of humor by becoming defensive or angry when someone laughs at them, even when the laughter is intended to form a connection and is not meant maliciously. For example, many of us have done something stupid and felt stupid when we realized what we had done but are able to laugh at ourselves. The destructive narcissist in this situation cannot laugh at him- or herself, cannot abide having others know that they did something stupid, and are very offended if others laugh.

Another example of the narcissist's lack of humor is their inability to see the humor in absurdities that may exist around them. At work it may be how absurd it is to continually reorganize, to constantly change direction, etc. While everyone else copes by laughing at the absurdities, this person does not see any humor in them.

Makes Sarcastic and Cutting Remarks

The person who constantly makes sarcastic and cutting remarks to coworkers is demonstrating a lack of respect and contempt for them. These remarks are intended to be devaluing, denigrating of others, and to demonstrate the speaker's superiority. They use sarcasm and cutting remarks to hurt others while pretending to be only joking. The other person is put in a bind because, if they respond in any way other than agreement with the remarks, they run the risk of being told they cannot take a joke, are overreacting, or that they are emotionally disturbed.

Sarcasm and cutting remarks are thinly disguised anger and hostility and will generate much resentment when employed as a consistent communication style. As with other destructive narcissistic characteristics, challenging, confronting, and attacking do not produce any positive change in the behavior. Quietly accepting this behavior usually results in considerable suppressed anger and resentment for those on the receiving end of the remarks, anger that tends to be manifested in physical ailments, reduced productivity, lowered morale, and other conditions detrimental to the work environment.

Tries to Intimidate

Coworkers and staff can be very uncomfortable with the person who tries to intimidate them but may not be able to explain just what the person is doing that produces the feeling of intimidation. One reason that identifying the specific behavior may be difficult is that there are verbal and nonverbal ways of trying to intimidate others. Some are not easily observed.

Some nonverbal behaviors that indicate a desire to intimidate can be categorized as invasion of the person's space. Specific acts such as leaning over the person, moving closer to individuals to the point where they move back or away, entering an office or workplace without knocking or waiting for permission, and sitting at either end of a table can be categorized as space invasion and aggression.

Some verbal behaviors that suggest intimidation are giving orders, making demeaning and criticizing remarks, talking loudly and rapidly, and interrupting. These are behaviors that have the goal of making the other person back away, feel inferior, and boost the status and power of the person using them.

Bosses seldom, if ever, experience these attempts at intimidation and for that reason may not be sensitive to complaints from others or even be aware of the behaviors. However, if coworkers and/or staff complain, it becomes easier to verify their perceptions by simply observing the person and asking the complainants to describe the behavior.

Attacks

Along with complaints about attempts to intimidate may be reports of feeling attacked. These feelings may be personal to the individual in the sense that this person tends to frequently feel attacked, even when no one else perceives them as being attacked. In this instance, the individual has personal issues and their feelings do not meet the test of objective reality.

On the other hand, if there are persistent reports from different people about feeling attacked by someone, this is an indication that the feelings are not individualized but do meet the test of objective reality. The attacking person is behaving in the manner described.

Attacks are not necessarily violent but they definitely indicate aggression. Usually the attacks are verbal, whereby the attacker is trying to assume power and superiority by demanding, criticizing, or putting the other person down, making others feel incompetent, stupid, inadequate, and inferior. The tone of voice can also indicate an attack, and the loud, rapid speech of a hostile, angry person can also be perceived as attacking.

There are also disguised ways of attacking, such as asking questions that are really statements. These are rhetorical questions where the questioner is trying to convey feelings (usually negative feelings), a different viewpoint, to criticize someone, and/or launch a defense. Questions such as, "Why do you think that?" can be disguised statements that are attacks where the questioner does not want to openly admit a personal viewpoint or is trying to devalue what is presented, all without having to assume personal responsibility for the act. The receiver tends to try to answer the question, which only leads to more questions and increased feelings of frustration.

Inflates Tasks, Contributions, and Accomplishments

Most everyone has a need or desire to feel that what they do is of importance and makes a worthwhile contribution. This is one of the ways that we give meaning to our lives. Feeling that what we are engaged in is of little or no importance promotes meaninglessness and despair, so it's understandable when an individual may sometimes exaggerate.

Destructive narcissists constantly inflate their tasks, contributions, and accomplishments. It seems that whatever they do is termed greater, more complex, more demanding, etc., than what others do. As you may know, this attitude and the accompanying behavior can promote much resentment among colleagues.

For example, this is the person who reports that they had to spend nights and weekends working on a project when, in fact, they did nothing of the sort. They may even have handed off much of the work to someone else while claiming credit for the job. They are also ignoring that others were in the same situation but are not talking about how much work they did.

There are numerous examples for this behavior, and it's not difficult for a boss to know when there is exaggeration. What bosses tend to ignore is the impact of this behavior on the rest of the workers. Even worse, they often buy into the inflation, inadvertently increasing resentment by others and promoting lowered morale.

Summary

You may find it unsettling to entertain the notion that you have a worker whose attitudes and behaviors reflect a destructive narcissistic pattern. But the negative effects on their coworkers, on the unit's productivity, and on morale is very real and should not be discounted. This chapter presented some reasons why you may perceive this person more positively than others do, and these reasons will call for some self-reflection and self-examination on your part if you are a boss. If you are this person's coworker, what was presented can help you better understand why the boss does not experience or perceive the destructive narcissist's negative behaviors and attitudes.

Chapter 7

Coping Strategies for the Boss

If you have identified a worker as a destructive narcissist or have sufficient reason to believe that there is one or more people in the unit who have destructive narcissistic characteristics, the task then becomes one of coping. What you do, how you do it, and what possible outcomes will result are vital considerations at this point. The task will be more complex and difficult because you may not have personal experience with some of the behaviors and attitudes that were reported to you, but can only infer what they were from their coworkers' reactions and the impact you see on the working environment. Further, remember that these workers' charm and attentiveness to you can produce a reluctance to believe that they are as destructive as these behaviors and attitudes would indicate. Even if you are not fully convinced that someone is a destructive narcissist, you can address the possibility and/or potential with the suggestions in this chapter.

Coping strategies for bosses are not tied necessarily to specific behaviors but are preventive and general. That is, your policies, guidelines for expected behaviors, and your own behaviors and attitude can do much to set a tone for a healthy working environment and eliminate or moderate the impact of a destructive narcissist. The first step is to take a personal inventory of your own possible underdeveloped narcissism. This step can help reduce any blind spots you may have and will increase your awareness of behaviors and attitudes indicative of underdeveloped narcissism in others.

Increase Your Personal Awareness

It's a difficult and continuing task to increase your awareness of personal behaviors, attitudes, and feelings that indicate underdeveloped narcissism. How much do you:

- seek or crave to be the center of attention, desire, or admiration;
- fail to recognize and respect others' boundaries;
- feel entitled to be treated special;
- exploit others;
- become impatient and irritated at displays of intense emotion by others;
- become arrogant or contemptuous and focus on others' shortcomings or faults;
- blame and criticize;
- inflate your accomplishments;
- boast or brag;
- believe others are envious of you, or should be envious;
- want to associate only with those who have power and status;
- feel that you make *"the* difference" and are crucial?

It is the rare person who does not have some lingering aspects of underdeveloped narcissism, and most remain unaware of how it's manifested in their present behaviors, attitudes, and feelings. They also do not recognize what impact it has on relationships and how it prevents recognizing similar characteristics in others, thereby reducing the ability to implement adequate prevention and coping strategies. The tendency for many bosses is to minimize or discount the impact of the worker's unrecognized underdeveloped or destructive narcissistic characteristics because the bosses would then have to accept that they too have the characteristics.

Use the items in the following scale to try and understand the underdeveloped narcissism in yourself that may be allowing you to overlook, ignore, rationalize, or minimize the reality and impact of the destructive narcissist's behavior on others. Look at the clusters of behaviors, attitudes, and feelings and do not focus on isolated ones. If your scores are above 50, you run the risk of not being able to see the destructiveness of the identified person because there are many similar characteristics. This tendency can be moderated some if you make a conscious effort to accept the observations and reports of the person's coworkers, not automatically spring to the person's defense, and do not ignore certain behaviors or excuse them.

Table 7.1: Personal Survey Scale

Directions: Rate yourself on each item using the scale below. Then, if you have an individual(s) you trust who often observes and interacts with you in the work environment, have that person(s) rate you separately. Remember, these are only suggestions.

5 – Almost always or always   2 – Seldom
4 – Frequently   1 – Almost never or never
3 – Sometimes   0 – Unable to rate or not applicable

I tend to:

1. become outraged when ignored

2. arrive late for meetings or leave early

3. sit at the head or foot of tables when not in charge of meetings

4. do the same things as those in power positions do, such as lunch in particular restaurants, patronize the same shops or tailor, etc.

5. engage in insincere flattery

6. enter workers' offices or work spaces without knocking

7. enter or sit down without an invitation from workers

8. put my arm around, pat, or touch workers without their permission

9. interrupt ongoing conversations

10. expect workers to do personal favors for me

11. feel that workers who display intense emotions are weak and/or out of control

12. make sure everyone knows how much work I have to do; how little help I get; etc.

13. give orders and expect them to be promptly carried out

14. think negatively about anyone who criticizes me

15. wonder why most other people are so incompetent

16. feel that the job would not get done if I did not constantly monitor everyone

17. become impatient or bored when workers tell me their personal problems

18. envy those who have more money, status, or power

19. fail to get satisfaction or pleasure from my accomplishments and/or possessions

20. have to always have the "biggest" and the "best"

21. feel that I deserve all the credit because nothing would get done if I did not see to it

22. when I am chastised, criticized or blamed, to know it was not my fault

23. not apologize for mistakes or errors

24. want to receive awards and other recognitions and am hurt when I do not

25. feel that I know best; have "the" answers

Scoring

100–125   You exhibit a considerable number of destructive narcissistic behaviors, attitudes, and feelings.

75–99   You exhibit many DN behaviors, attitudes, and feelings.

50–74   You exhibit some DN behaviors, attitudes, and feelings.

25–49   You seldom exhibit DN behaviors, attitudes, and feelings.

It's easier to become aware of how others display destructive narcissistic characteristics than it is to see personal underdeveloped narcissism. Our own underdeveloped narcissism is a part of us that is often much more obvious to others than it is to us, even though it continues to affect our behaviors, attitudes, feelings, and relationships. However, the less you are aware of your personal underdeveloped narcissistic behaviors, attitudes, and feelings, the more you will be inclined to overlook or rationalize them in the destructive narcissist, and the more open you will be to manipulation by this person. There are several motivators for working to develop your underdeveloped narcissism:

- you can reduce the potential for manipulation,

- your capacity for forming and maintaining meaningful relationships can increase,

- your ability to be empathic is expanded, and

- your creativity can be fostered.

Increasing your awareness of destructive narcissistic behaviors and attitudes can aid you, as the boss, to more clearly perceive and understand what may be happening in the workplace. For example, you can better understand why morale is low or why productivity is stagnant or decreased, why good people are leaving or want to leave, why workers are suspicious of each other, etc. A destructive narcissist who is unrecognized and unchecked can produce any and all of these undesirable conditions. Once you are aware of the destructive narcissist you can implement steps to lessen their impact on their coworkers.

You do not have to believe or accept that you have any destructive narcissistic characteristics in order to use effective strategies for coping with a self-absorbed worker. You only have to be willing to consider the idea that you may be overlooking, ignoring, or minimizing some of their behaviors and attitudes and that your indifference can have a demoralizing and detrimental effect on your unit resulting in lowered productivity. Why you choose to rationalize or ignore their behavior is not nearly as important as your willingness to take steps to moderate the impact of their behavior on coworkers. You can both consider the person in question to be charming, personable, and positive and institute policies and personal behaviors that will benefit their coworkers.

Acceptance

The next step is your acceptance that what is being reported or observed is mostly accurate, negative effects are being felt, your experience of the person is different, and/or preventive measures can be helpful. It's not easy to trust that reports of events you do not personally observe or experience are accurate. It's much easier to consider the complaints and negative effects the results of misunderstandings, overreaction or hypersensitivity, competition, and/or personality conflicts, especially since these could be real possible explanations. However, when several workers have the same experiences, similar complaints and feelings, report continuing frustrations, etc., you should entertain the notion that what they are reporting is accurate. The boss needs to remember that what is being reported are not isolated incidents but experiences over time, that coworkers are reluctant to come to you with complaints, and that they do so out of an inability to solve the problem themselves. There is the further constraint that much of what the destructive narcissist does is difficult to describe to someone else who does not experience the person in the same way.

You will also have to accept that you will not be able to change the destructive narcissist. You can insist on certain behaviors, but nothing you do or say will effect a lasting change. An important aspect of acceptance for you is the realization that you are limited in what you will be able to accomplish. Even if you have a sincere desire to help the person overcome their underdeveloped narcissism, you are limited to insisting on specific behavioral changes. It may be humbling to realize just how limited your options are, but it's very necessary that you overcome any lingering aspects of grandiosity you may have and accept that you cannot change the destructive narcissist; you can only moderate their impact.

Review the Work Environment

The next step is to take a look at your management style and determine if it encourages some of these destructive narcissistic behaviors. Your management style has a significant impact on the work environment. For example, you may favor an informal management style where everyone, including you, is expected to have an open-door policy. However, this style may be encouraging extensive boundary violations where the self-absorbed person feels free to interrupt others, borrow or take their belongings, and/or enter their space without asking or waiting for permission.

Another example is seen in a more formal management style, where the boss remains somewhat detached and aloof. Under these circumstances attention and praise from the boss is coveted and the destructive narcissist will actively pursue getting this attention by demeaning, devaluing, and disparaging coworkers to make themselves look better. The boss may be too much removed from workers to know what's really happening.

These are but two examples out of many possible ones, but they serve to illustrate how aspects of a management style can allow the destructive narcissist to operate. Identifying your management style can help suggest appropriate strategies. You can then choose strategies that are most consistent with your management style.

Following are some suggested strategies together with rationales and possible outcomes. This is not an exhaustive list—at best it's only a beginning. In addition, strategies must be used that fit both the needs of the workplace and the personality of the boss. This is another reason for the boss to do a personal survey, as self-understanding helps in making choices of strategies.

Table 7-2: Coping Strategies for the Boss

1. Listen carefully to what subordinates tell you.

2. Maintain appropriate boundaries:

   * Separate social activities from professional ones,

   * Do not play favorites,

   * Do not ask for favors, especially personal ones,

3. Refuse to join in negative comments.

4. Distribute praise and approval equally.

5. Be very clear about expectations, evaluation, and procedures.

6. Focus on solutions—not blame.

7. Provide for sufficient and appropriate recognition for all work done.

8. Monitor distribution of workload.

9. Increase awareness of DN behaviors and personal underdeveloped narcissism.

10. Realize and accept that you cannot change them but can only moderate the impact of their behavior.

11. Model appropriate behaviors.

12. Block blaming, criticizing, demeaning, devaluing, and disparaging comments.

13. Do not encourage familiarity—recognize your power, status, and responsibility.

14. Put it in writing—directions, assignments, requests, and policies.

Listen Carefully

Listening is a skill that cannot be underestimated in its usefulness. The ability to hear what another person is saying and understand what they mean fosters positive communication and reduces misunderstandings. This is the skill that can help you realize the impact of a destructive narcissist's behavior and tune in to when someone is displaying self-absorbed behaviors and attitudes.

Realizing the impact of these behaviors and attitudes is a wake-up call that productivity and morale are negatively affected. Listening to what workers are saying and meaning can help the boss understand that destructive narcissism is playing a part in making the work environment uncomfortable and unpleasant.

Listening involves hearing words and understanding meanings. It includes being able to tune in to direct and indirect expressions of feelings. The indirect and nonverbal part of communications are the most important, as they carry the "real" message. The words used are not nearly as important as the feelings behind them. An example is when a worker makes a comment to the boss about working on a project without receiving any credit. The worker may say, mildly in a passing conversation, that they and others contributed to the project and wrote the findings but that only the destructive narcissist's name was on the project report. The real message might be that they are frustrated and angry at receiving no credit and frustrated with you, the boss, for accepting the destructive narcissist at face value and not realizing that the person is taking all the credit. If the boss allows this state of affairs to continue by not hearing the real message, productivity will suffer.

Maintain Appropriate Boundaries

Boundaries and the need for firm, clear ones are presented in depth in chapter 9, so the discussion here will focus on a general approach that can prevent some distressing behaviors from becoming problems that affect morale and productivity.

Appropriate boundaries for bosses include:

- separating personal activities from professional activities,
- making clear the distinction between personal social activities and professional social ones,
- not playing favorites,
- not asking for favors, and
- not encouraging casual negative comments about coworkers.

The most effective thing a boss can do in setting appropriate boundaries is to separate professional activities from personal and social activities. While there are also social activities that are professionally related, the boss should have a clear understanding of the distinction. Personal and professional can overlap at times, but these overlaps should be kept to a minimum.

This suggestion does not mean that the boss should be detached and aloof from workers, never mingling or sharing social activities. However, it does mean that the boss should be very clear that these social activities are professional in nature and not an invitation to personal intimacy. It's much more difficult to accept criticism, even constructive criticism, and an evaluation less than excellent from someone you think is a friend than it is to accept these from someone who is trying to be objective as a part of the job description. Maintaining professional boundaries help both the worker and the boss.

This suggestion can be particularly useful because the destructive narcissist is not easily identified as such and may go undetected for some time. If appropriate professional boundaries are already in place, then the boss lessens the risk of being manipulated or fooled by the self-absorbed person. Further, the impact of the destructive narcissist on the unit is moderated because this person cannot claim a social or more intimate relationship with the boss.

Do Not Play Favorites

A strategy that is helpful in maintaining appropriate boundaries is to avoid playing favorites. This may not be as easy to do as it sounds because some people are more personable, likable, and charming than others and it's easy to favor those over the person who does not have these pleasing qualities. However, it is extremely demoralizing when the boss appears to favor some people, or even one person.

Being perceived as unique and special is a desire of the destructive narcissist who may also have the expectation of being the boss's favorite. This person will engage in activities and behaviors to highlight similarities with the boss and use every opportunity to try and gain an advantage. It can be very difficult for a boss (or for anyone), to differentiate sincerity from insincerity, and the destructive narcissist capitalizes on this.

The boss should make every effort to be evenhanded in distributing both criticism and praise attempting to see that everyone gets praise and everyone who merits it gets appropriate, constructive criticism.

Do Not Ask for Favors

Another strategy that helps maintain appropriate boundaries is to have policy of not requesting any favors from workers, especially personal favors. If you have a destructive narcissistic person in your unit that has been identified as such, you may also want to get in the habit of not doing favors, except those that are a part of your professional responsibilities.

I'm suggesting this behavior and attitude because destructive narcissists still have some unresolved issues around separation and individuation (see chapter 2). They will tend to see others as extensions of self and under their control. This tendency, paired with a sense of entitlement, can produce unreasonable expectations that are fueled when others do favors for them or when those with status and power request favors. The simple request for a favor by the boss becomes very complicated when dealing with destructive narcissists, as they can then assume that they are being singled out as superior to others, are considered by the boss to be unique and special, and are entitled to special treatment and consideration.

Refuse to Join in Negative Comments

A very simple coping strategy is to refuse to accept or contribute to criticizing, blaming, demeaning, or disparaging comments. Agreeing with these kind of comments is encouraging and leads to a belief that the target of these comments is inferior and the commentator is superior. When a boss agrees with or adds to these negative comments, either verbally or nonverbally, any idea of fair and equitable treatment for workers in the unit has been destroyed.

Saying nothing can be misunderstood, as some people perceive silence as agreement. Expected behavior is much clearer when bosses will directly say that they have no intention of joining in blaming or criticizing others for problems, and that they prefer to look for solutions.

This, of course, does not mean that the boss should not listen to complaints and factual reports about workers in their unit. The boss should listen and, if these people are making errors, setting up roadblocks, etc., to address these behaviors as constraints on productivity. Listening carefully to legitimate, factual complaints is also one way to begin to realize that there is a destructive narcissist in the unit.

What is important to remember is that the destructive narcissist displays a cluster of behaviors and attitudes and this behavior of making negative comments is only one of them. However, if you discourage negative comments by refusing to join in when they are made, you've found one way to curb the destructive narcissist's behavior.

Distribute Praise and Approval

It may take a conscious effort by the boss to make sure that praise and approval are somewhat equally distributed. That is, recognition of efforts and outcome should be given to all who deserve it, not just one or two individuals.

The destructive narcissist can have an inordinate need for admiration and expend considerable time and effort to obtain it. I don't mean that they work hard earning it, but they make sure they're at the forefront of every opportunity for praise, emphasizing his or her accomplishments, downplaying the contributions of others, etc. A boss can unintentionally encourage this behavior and further demoralize workers by frequently giving this person what they are looking for by praising them and neglecting to praise others for the same kinds of things.

For example, let's say you have a destructive narcissistic coworker who expects and pursues admiration. The boss tends to play into this behavior by praising this person for doing this, that, or the other thing but does not praise anyone else for anything. It does not take long for workers to perceive the boss as playing favorites, which makes them feel that their efforts are unrecognized and unappreciated. This can lead to decreased morale and poor productivity.

Make Your Expectations Clear

Ambiguity and uncertainty produce considerable anxiety, fear, and dread. Almost everyone feels more confident and assured when they know what is expected and can better judge their abilities and competencies to meet these expectations. When expectations are vague or unspecified, anxiety is increased, leading to conditions that can be exploited by a destructive narcissist.

The situation can be exploited because of several behaviors and attitudes of these people. For example, they tend to assume that they are in charge (grandiosity) and have the right to give orders (entitlement). When there are no clear guidelines for what is to be done and who is to do what, this person begins to off-load work and responsibilities on others. If challenged, they'll say that they're just fostering teamwork or trying to provide leadership, but what is actually happening is that they are riding roughshod over their coworkers.

The boss can prevent this state of affairs from occurring by being very specific in what is expected. Written directions and guidelines for the workplace should not be open to interpretation but should be clear to all who read them. It may be helpful for the boss to reduce or eliminate verbal instructions or orders, as these can more easily be misunderstood.

Along with clarity of expectations, the boss needs to be very clear about evaluation criteria and procedures. Workers are understandably anxious about these, as they can seriously impact their career and life. Ambiguous criteria also do not allow workers to know what they are expected to do or the level to which they should perform. While some can argue that ambiguity about expectations produces necessary tension—keeping everyone on their toes—it is hard to see how this tension contributes to a positive work environment.

Focus on Solutions, Not Blame

Destructive narcissists are prone to blame others and to make sure that they have to assume as little responsibility as possible for their errors. Without worrying about who is at fault when things go awry, a boss would be more constructive to focus on solutions.

A focus on solutions means that you maintain the attitude that everyone makes mistakes and that criticizing them for the mistake is less helpful that trying to understand how it occurred so that steps can be taken to insure that such a mistake is unlikely to occur again. For example, there may be instances when a mistake occurred because of a lack of information or because the person received some misinformation. Instead of blaming the person who failed to get the needed information across, steps could be taken to facilitate the flow of relevant information to the person who needs it. That person is then most likely to feel that they are not being judged as incompetent and their self-efficacy will not suffer.

The boss who adopts this attitude is modeling for everyone how to get the job done, increasing morale, promoting an attitude among workers of looking for solutions to errors rather than hiding them or off-loading them, and demonstrating how to effectively solve problems. The impact of a destructive narcissist in this situation is decreased.

Provide Sufficient and Equal Recognition

Using this suggestion may involve a little more effort on your part. It takes attention to provide for sufficient and appropriate recognition for all work done. A boss needs to be aware of what is being done and by whom to judge the quality of the work and provide proper recognition.

The destructive narcissist thrives in an environment where only stars receive recognition because then it becomes much easier to gain the status of being considered unique and special. It's easier because they can be charming when necessary and will play up to the boss, denigrate their coworkers, and inflate their accomplishments so that they appear to be the stars, regardless of the actual work they've performed. A boss under these circumstances is usually so dazzled, charmed, and manipulated that they cannot see what is happening to them and to the other workers. By remaining vigilant in distributing praise and recognition equally and fairly, you can derail this kind of manipulation.

Monitor Distribution of the Workload

As I've mentioned before, some destructive narcissists will go to great lengths to get their coworkers to do their work. This is why it can be so important for a boss to monitor the workload, ensuring they know who is doing what, whether they were actually assigned to this task, and if they have the resources to complete the job.

Giving assignments in writing is less likely to be distorted than when assignments are verbal. Even more prone to distortion is when verbal assignments are not given directly but through another person. For example, the boss tells Jim to get Mary to help him with the assignment. If Jim is a destructive narcissist, he may order Mary to do certain tasks, and if she protests he will then tell her that the boss said she had to do it. Mary then begins to feel put upon and bewildered, losing confidence that she is considered competent since the boss did not directly tell her what he wanted her to do. Or Jim may off-load the entire job on Mary, again telling her that this is what the boss wanted. It is unlikely that Mary will go to the boss to clarify what was really said and, even if she does, the boss may then consider her to be a tattletale and not a team player, or she may fear that this will be the reaction.

By no means does monitoring mean micromanaging. Monitoring simply means paying attention and being aware. Micromanaging means that workers are not being allowed to do the job in the way that makes sense to them but are having to work by the boss's dictate of how it must be done. Monitoring gives workers some structure and direction without stifling their creativity and enthusiasm.

Accept Your Limitations

Accepting that you cannot change the destructive narcissist can be very humbling and difficult. The reality is that, at best, you will only be able to moderate their impact on their coworkers. However, even that little bit can be good enough to keep morale and productivity at acceptable levels.

Your first inclination may be to talk with the person about their behaviors and attitudes with the expectation that if you confront them, they will understand what they are doing and change. *Confrontation is not a strategy that is effective with a destructive narcissist.* Because you are the boss, the person will appear to agree with you, but you're not likely to observe any meaningful changes. This person will make excuses, blame and criticize others, misunderstand and distort what you say, and/or become offended. These reactions occur because destructive narcissists do not have the capacity to understand what others are experiencing. They feel they are *entitled* to manipulate and exploit others. They cannot recognize or understand boundaries and therefore fail to understand what others may object to. Because you, as the boss, are in a power position, they will try to impress you. For these and other reasons, the first inclination you may have to talk with them about changing their behavior will seldom produce meaningful outcomes. The other suggestions discussed in this chapter will produce more durable results as they are predicated on the basis of accepting that you cannot change the destructive narcissist.

Model Appropriate Behaviors

One effective way to prevent and block undesirable destructive narcissistic behaviors is for the boss to model appropriate behaviors. The boss can:

- look for solutions rather than blaming,

- help workers capitalize on their strengths instead of criticizing,

- give workers credit instead of taking all of the credit for their work or contributions,

- respect boundaries such as worker's personal workplace by knocking and waiting for permission to enter,

- prepare and disseminate guidelines that describe expectations and evaluation procedures,

- refuse to listen to disparaging comments but be willing to listen to concerns that have a basis in objective behaviorally based reality, and

- show respect and appreciation for individuality.

A boss does not have to be perfect to model appropriate behaviors, just have an awareness of what they are and a personal commitment to behave in accord with them.

Taking a personal inventory is the first step. Review the list of behaviors in chapter 3, "The Destructive Narcissistic Boss" to determine which behaviors are frequent. It can also be helpful to check out some of your self-perceptions with another person who can be trusted to be honest (but tactful) in their appraisal. Once you can identify some behaviors to reduce, eliminate, or institute, you are well on your way to modeling appropriate behaviors.

For example, suppose you realize that you do tend to criticize workers quite often. You may feel that you do this in an effort to help them improve, eliminate mistakes, and/or communicate your expectations. All of these are worthwhile objectives but may have unintended outcomes, such as workers feeling devalued or experiencing lowered morale or a loss of self-confidence. Also, bear in mind that a critical environment will encourage manipulation from the destructive narcissistic worker. Once you are aware of this tendency you can make a conscious effort to keep from making criticizing comments and to institute more constructive ways of accomplishing your objectives.

Block Negative Remarks

Another strategy is to block any remarks that are blaming, criticizing, demeaning, devaluing, or disparaging. Many times these comments are indirect, subtle, or offhand and the tendency is either to ignore them if you disagree or to verbally or nonverbally agree with the comment. If you ignore them it may be assumed that you agree with the comment since many people believe that silence indicates consent or agreement. Even a head nod or grunt can be viewed as agreement.

However, it's much more constructive when the boss blocks such comments. Blocking sends a message that this is unacceptable behavior and that the boss does not appreciate hearing these comments. Workers who know that the boss is not receptive to these comments can begin to feel more respected and valued, no longer afraid that the boss is looking for scapegoats. These positive results can lead to a high level of morale and a more congenial work environment. The focus is on constructive solutions, not on assigning blame or establishing a hierarchy of approval.

Blocking all such comments can be a useful strategy for all bosses but is particularly useful when there is a destructive narcissist in the unit. This person will need to be perceived as superior, unique, and special and will engage in these comments to attain the boss's approval and to insure that the boss perceives him or her as superior and others as inferior. Blocking reduces the possibility that you may be influenced by unwarranted negative comments. Even when bosses try to be objective they can be unconsciously influenced by hearing negative comments that are sometimes so indirect that it is difficult to openly challenge them.

How do you block these comments? One effective way to block is to respond to each comment and innuendo by ignoring the content and saying that you prefer to focus on positives and solutions. It can also be useful to ask the person making the comment if they have any constructive solutions. In other words, do not ignore these comments but respond directly and firmly. Another strategy can be to say that you think you understand what the person is trying to convey but do not consider it useful to continue to explore the topic. These are two ways of blocking when interacting on an individual basis.

When these comments start to surface in a group setting, such as during a meeting, they can be blocked by immediately interrupting and saying that you want the focus to be on solutions. Or you can comment that you would prefer to hear what is being done to correct problems, that you do not intend to let anyone be the scapegoat, or that such comments are out of line. You will probably only have to do this once in a group for everyone to receive the message.

One final strategy is to openly express appreciation and approval when someone assumes responsibility for a mistake and institutes steps to either correct the mistake or insure that it will not happen again. Workers then begin to believe that the boss does focus on solutions.

Do Not Encourage Familiarity

An important boundary that is often overlooked or discounted is the one between the boss and everyone else. Some bosses try to blur the boundary in order not to appear aloof and superior. Others genuinely feel that they are on the same level as everyone else, just in a different position. Whatever the reason for wanting to be considered just another member of the team, doing so can be a mistake when working with a destructive narcissist.

Why would this be a mistake? There are several possible negative outcomes that could occur, and most, if not all, could be prevented if the boundary were maintained. When you blur this boundary you may in effect be inviting the destructive narcissist to try to cozy up to you, making negative comments about their coworkers and giving the impression to others that they are your favorite. It can appear that this person is being favored because he or she is taking liberties that the boss does not know about, communicates lies and distortions that are attributed to the boss; and because the boss is known to treat workers as coworkers, these become more believable.

Trying to correct any of these conditions or perceptions is extremely difficult and time consuming. Preventing them takes little effort and suggested strategies may be appropriate even when not having to deal with a destructive narcissist.

The first strategy is to recognize and accept your position as one of power, status, and responsibility. The boss is part of the team, but also has a very different role to play. It's more helpful to everyone when the boss does not consider him or herself to be superior but does recognize the differences in position and behaves accordingly. A boss usually has the final word or significant input into raises, promotions, hiring, and firing of workers. This is a position of considerable power even when there are procedures for disagreeing with the boss's decision. A boss also either does an evaluation of a worker's productivity or, again, has significant input into the evaluation. These are all reasons why it's important for a boss to recognize and accept their position. These are not all of the reasons but serve as examples.

Another strategy is easier to initiate when the boss first begins at a workplace. That is, to use formality as the structure for interacting. Too much formality makes workers feel stifled, but having some formality helps maintain boundaries. Formal structures include using titles (Mr. or Ms. or Mrs.), transacting important business by making appointments rather than simply having impromptu conversations, and limiting the exchange of personal information, concerns, or issues. Some degree of formality shows respect and helps maintain boundaries without conveying an attitude of aloofness and superiority.

The last suggested strategy is to cultivate an air of friendliness but not to try and be a pal. Pals are on equal footing, and the boss is not an equal. Further, being a pal leaves you open to hearing inappropriate comments, and may encourage some to take liberties, assume special status, and believe that rules and regulations either do not apply or will be relaxed. While none of this may be the actual state of affairs, your friendliness can easily be misunderstood and can be almost impossible to correct.

Put It in Writing

Communication in writing is a very powerful strategy when dealing with a destructive narcissist. Writing down your decisions, guidelines, assignments, requests, and policies can prevent many misunderstandings, distortions, and lies. Further, by writing these you then have a record if they are ever called into question. Writing also prevents a destructive narcissist from speaking for you, which some try to do in order to be considered unique and special or out of their grandiose notion that they are in charge, their attitude of entitlement, and/or their attitude of superiority.

The boss who communicates important things in writing underscores their importance and gives workers something tangible for referral. This, of course, does not eliminate dialogue, which certainly can then be used for clarification and elaboration but isn't the best foundation to use with a destructive narcissist. Further, valuable time is not used to correct misunderstandings and misperceptions, as these become fewer. While most everything can be open to interpretation, a boss will find that there is likely to be more commonality in understanding what is meant when it's provided in writing. The most important outcome is prevention of the destructive narcissist's negative impact on colleagues.

Summary

It was stated previously that the coping strategies for the boss that are presented in this chapter are intended to be general and preventative. If you are a boss, you will find it less effective to institute these strategies as changes and remedial than it is to have them as your usual professional expectations and demeanor. Remediation can be done, but it is not easily accomplished. These strategies can work, are effective, and can moderate or eliminate many negative effects of the destructive narcissist. Further, you will not have to identify a particular person as having a destructive narcissistic pattern as you have organized your professional expectations and demeanor to apply to everyone. That allows everyone to see that your treatment of workers is intended to be fair and objective.

Chapter 8

Effects of the Destructive Narcissist on the Unit or Team

Effects on the Group

Units, teams, departments, etc., are groups, and prolonged contact with a destructive narcissist generally leads to a negative impact on the group as a whole. When bosses or supervisors are destructive narcissists, their impact is more widespread and intensive than that for a worker. However, do not underestimate the extent of the negative impact of the destructive narcissist worker, as it can be considerable.

It's much easier to see and understand the impact on individuals than it is to understand how the distressing behaviors and attitudes impact the unit, team, or department as a whole. The difficulty arises in part from the tendency to focus on individuals and their reactions. Another difficulty is that the "group" is not generally perceived as an entity having specific characteristics. This discussion focuses on the group and is based on the assumption that the group is more than a collection of individuals—it is also a system that incorporates and synthesizes individual characteristics.

One example of what I mean by the group entity can be seen in the output of a cohesive group. When members of a cohesive group work together to produce a product, solve a problem, develop a process, etc., the outcome is superior to that for an individually produced outcome. Johnson and Johnson (1996) note that the results of a meta-analysis of 120 studies on the effectiveness of team productivity versus individual productivity points to the overwhelming superiority of the team effort. Each individual contributes, but the result is usually a cut above being just a collection of individual contributions.

The following presents an example of what happened when a work group tried to cope with a member who was a destructive narcissist. But, before presenting the example, it may be useful to review the characteristics of a cohesive and productive group as the impact of the destructive narcissist can be better perceived in this context.

Cohesive and Productive Groups

Johnson and Johnson list the following as characteristics of cohesive groups.

- Goals are more easily determined.

- The group is more likely to achieve these goals.

- Members demonstrate more commitment to the group and its task.

- There is less absenteeism.

- Turnover decreases.

- Members assume personal responsibility for the group and its outcomes.

- There is increased willingness to take on more difficult tasks.

- Motivation and persistence in achieving goals is high.

- There is a willingness to defend the group.

- There is a willingness to listen to and be influenced by coworkers.

- There is a sense of solidarity.

- Members value the group and provide mutual support for each other.

- Controversy and conflict are allowed to emerge and are constructively resolved.

- Morale is high.

- There is mutual trust among members.

A Group with a Destructive Narcissist

The following description is based on a true event but names and other identifying data were changed.

The group that is the focus for this example is composed of professionals, most of whom worked in the particular setting for several years. The majority of members had worked together for over ten years and most of them were very knowledgeable about the work and various policies. When John was named the department head by the dean, there was some apprehension but only to the extent that he was new in a leadership position and members of the department did not know what to expect.

Prior to John being named head, the unit had many characteristics that describe a cohesive group. There was agreement on goals, even though individuals differed in their perceptions of how best to attain these goals. Members were committed to the group and its task as evidenced by high productivity, little turnover, and very little absenteeism. Members assumed responsibility readily, took on difficult tasks with little or no grumbling, were willing to listen to each other and make compromises, and were mutually supportive. The group was not free of controversy and conflict, but when conflict did emerge, considerable efforts were expended on the part of all parties concerned to arrive at a mutually agreeable solution. The group tended to make decisions by consensus and tried to do so on most occasions. While conditions were not perfect, as a group they worked well together.

Immediately upon assuming the position, John began to unilaterally make extensive changes and to give orders. For example he:

- restructured the work of the support staff so that group members no longer received any of the usual services,

- moved the main office of a program without any prior notice to the people it served,

- began to berate group members about minor things, such as how many sheets of paper they used to reproduce needed materials, and

- had the locks changed for the main office and refused to give group members keys whereas previously they had had keys to the office.

Impact of the DN on the Group

All these actions had a significant impact on productivity. For example, a considerable amount of work was usually done outside of regular hours and not having keys made that impossible. In addition, even though John should have been familiar with policies and procedures, he made decisions and carried out activities that were in contradiction to written policies and procedures, resulting in considerable confusion and misunderstandings.

Any time a group member tried to talk with him, John would make unfounded accusations, and criticisms, engage in fault-finding, and spread lies and confusion. Somehow, every conversation resulted in the other person being blamed for something by John. It did not matter what he or she was blamed for, whether it was of some consequence or a very minor matter, everyone was told in no uncertain terms that they were at fault for something. Even when the conversation was about something positive, John found some way to turn it around so that there was something negative expressed about the person.

This state of affairs went on for some time, as most members interacted with him on an individual basis and kept secret their feelings of frustration, anger, and confusion. There was a lot of self-blaming, with people feeling that they had failed to live up to expected standards and that if they just tried a little harder they could please John and understand him.

The impact on the group was felt through some of the following feelings and behaviors:

- decreased empathy,
- increased withdrawal,
- refusal to participate,
- more absenteeism,
- less commitment to the group and less willingness to defend the group,
- resistance to listen to and be influenced by other group members,
- increased irritability,
- decreased productivity,

- emerging conflicts not dealt with in a constructive way,

- more masking of feelings along with frequent inappropriate expressions of feelings, and

- lowered morale.

Decreased Empathy

This particular group had previously displayed a high degree of empathy. When conflicts had occurred, each member tried hard to understand the other person's perspective and feelings. Members were respectful of others' feelings and paid particular attention to how they expressed negative feelings, using constructive confrontation and feedback techniques. When the group ran into a conflict, members demonstrated a responsible and mature way of handling it.

After John assumed control, members displayed much less empathy for each other. It was as if they did not care what the other person felt, becoming careless about how they expressed negative feelings. Group members became more detached and aloof, paying little attention to feelings and focusing on thoughts to the exclusion of feelings.

Increased Withdrawal

Gradually, members of the group began to withdraw from interactions with John and with each other. The withdrawal took many forms, such as developing elaborate schemes to reduce unexpected encounters with him because these encounters usually resulted in his criticizing, berating, finding fault, or some other unpleasant experience.

John was also adept at playing one member against another. One example of this is when he would invite comments about someone by making a negative comment or observation about the person. The receivers generally listened to him and would agree because they felt he had observed the person over a long time. The receiver would often find themselves agreeing with the negative comment or seeming to agree to keep from becoming a target of John's displeasure.

It did not take long for members of the group to realize that when they agreed with John's negative comment, he would waste little time in reporting it back to the original person, except that he would explain that is was his coworker's opinion, not his. The way John managed this was to suggest that the person had come to John to specifically make these negative comments. Sometimes the negativity was exaggerated in the retelling. For example, John commented that so-and-so seemed irritable, but in the retelling he said that the person was described by someone else as always irritated and contentious. Group members gradually became very suspicious of each other as everyone was the target of a negative comment as well as being charged with making these comments. Members did not challenge each other about what was said but began to limit contact with each other. They also felt they had to be very careful in what they said to each other in fear of their comments being repeated, distorted, or misunderstood. Withdrawal was the method of choice as a defense.

Refusal to Participate

Members used every excuse in the book to try and do as little as possible. Since members did have some say so in deciding which tasks to do, they used their privilege to say no whenever possible. Indeed, even when they ended up having to do a task, the initial request to do it was met with a refusal, or considerable reluctance.

John became very frustrated that group members were not rushing to volunteer to do tasks. His expectation was that members would want his approval and attention so much that they would compete for it. And at first there was some of this competition when group members assumed that John would be similar to the previous department heads and because members wanted to be positively perceived. While members did not know that John had numerous destructive narcissistic characteristics, they eventually learned that they were more likely to get devaluing and depreciation from him than they were to get approval. Attention from John usually resulted in something negative, and so members avoided this negativity by refusing to participate whenever possible.

More Absenteeism

Members used every imaginable excuse to be absent from meetings with John. Some even went so far as to volunteer for other committee assignments as these committee meetings meant that they would have to miss group meetings where John was present. Other excuses such as illness, previous commitments, traffic, and absent-mindedness were also used. There was no collusion—each person just developed their own excuse to be as far from John as possible.

Members managed to miss attending meetings in a way that was not obvious unless you were aware that previously there had been very little absenteeism. Of course, part of the reason for increased absenteeism could have been the increase in the number and frequency of meetings. John more than doubled the number of meetings for the unit.

Less Commitment

One indication of less commitment to the group was the reluctance to suggest or participate in new initiatives. Some activities that members had previously seemed to value were dropped for lack of interest, and appeals to members to do things that would further the aims of the group appeared to fall on deaf ears. This is not to say that members refused to do their jobs or many job-related tasks—they continued to perform in a professional and responsible manner. What did occur was a considerable lack of enthusiasm for taking on anything but basic, essential tasks and a reluctance or refusal to go beyond basic requirements for maintenance of the unit. Members found outlets for their creativity and enthusiasm outside the group rather than making these contributions to the group.

Another indicator was the decrease in member's willingness to defend the group. Members who previously would leap to the group's defense now kept quiet. Defending the group was second nature before because other group members could be counted on to provide support and encouragement. This was no longer the case because John had stirred up suspicion and distrust among group members and no one could be sure they would be supported if they attempted to defend the group. Also, it became almost impossible to mount a defense against attacks by him.

Resistance to Other Group Members

Members of the group became increasingly resistant to listen to and be influenced by each other. This made it difficult to obtain consensus, and more decisions were made by majority vote. This led to many more members being on a losing side. Where before, members had been willing to consider differing perspectives and work to effect compromises, they increasingly took a stand on issues and refused to be swayed by any input from other members.

Further evidence of becoming resistant to other group members was seen in the increased withdrawal from interaction between members. Members did not refuse to interact, they just limited the amount and time of interacting. For example, instead of informal meetings of several group members, there were instances of two or three members interacting briefly but seldom on anything of importance. No effort was made to include others in these meetings to make sure they were inclusive.

Even junior members were reluctant to listen to and be influenced by other group members who were more senior and experienced. Meetings became very tense because most all members took a position and refused to compromise and no particular efforts were made to be supportive of one another. There was general suspicion that all comments were being reported to John, so few were willing to be candid in expressing their opinions. There was ample reason to believe that comments were being reported along with identification of who made the comment, as John would drop hints that indicated he knew what had been said and by whom. No one was sure who could be trusted and who was carrying tales, and so each remained isolated and resistant to being influenced by anyone.

Increased Irritability

Small irritations began to grate and people were more inclined to allow them to influence their words and actions. In short, people became cranky, and even though almost everyone made conscious efforts to control their reactions to these minor irritations, they were not completely successful. It seemed easier to say or do something that irritated the other person, and it seemed that they, too, were doing and saying things that were more irritating.

A part of the irritability arose from the perception that what others said and did probably had a hidden agenda and that they could or would report everything to John. He would then turn around and use the information in a way that would be detrimental to the person. So, members became irritated because of the lack of trust and safety in the group. No one knew who could be trusted and who could not.

Increased irritability was also evidenced by members' whining, carping, criticizing, and blaming. It seemed as if no one was ever pleased, satisfied, or appreciative of anything or by anyone. Members compensated by reducing contact with each other.

Decreased Productivity

The decrease in productivity was minimal but enough to be detectable, and when that decrease is added to the failure to grow or increase in line with previous years, the overall downward slide was considerable. Members continued to do their essential or basic jobs but did not go further. Some even openly identified what tasks they considered to be basic and gave many reasons why they would not go beyond these. The lack of initiatives and creativity was very apparent.

No Constructive Conflict Resolution

Members of this particular group had been very good in using constructive confrontation skills. That is, they:

- used active listening skills,

- focused on behavior,

- invited the person to examine the behavior and its impact on the confronter rather than demanded that they do so,

- stayed aware of the feelings generated in both the giver and receiver of the confrontation and did not allow them to intensify or escalate,

- timed the confrontation appropriately, and

- used extensive clarifying and feedback skills.

However, after John was appointed department head, members seemed to forget to use their expertise in conflict resolution. Conflicts that previously would have been worked out in a way that was satisfactory to all concerned parties were suppressed or allowed to escalate into animosity and verbal fights. Most all members had at least one shouting match with John, and many had more than one. More members had shouting matches with each other, especially over somewhat small matters. Some conflicts between members were the result of displaced feelings generated by the boss. The important point is that when conflicts emerged, members no longer put the effort in to solve them constructively.

Masking and Inappropriate Expressions of Feelings

When you fail to use constructive conflict resolution strategies, you can easily begin to slip into inappropriate expression of feelings. Engaging in shouting matches and having arguments where one or both members become angry are not behaviors associated with appropriate feeling expression for the workplace.

Of more concern is the extent to which members of this group tried to mask their feelings. For example, members used to be open to hearing diverse opinions, but after John had been department head for a while, the group seemed closed but did not openly disagree or even try to get clarification or obtain consensus. Input was reduced as members were reluctant to advance ideas and opinions. Silence became the norm, and when someone did speak there was little or no direct response from other group members.

Masking could also be seen in members' tendency to withdraw from contact with each other. Little socializing occurred, and members voted against any kind of celebrations such as a holiday party at the end of the year. Even between those members who previously had cordial relationships and considered each other friends, there was reduced openness and expression of feelings.

Lowered Morale

All members at some time expressed disappointment and discontent. The overall tone for the unit was one of depression. Lowered morale was characterized by:

- disorganization,

- apathy,

- aimlessness,

- lack of purpose and sense of meaninglessness, and

- little concern for the future.

The healthy bond of meaningfulness and commitment to the unit and job was broken, and group members acutely felt the loss.

As you can see, this destructive narcissistic boss had a considerable impact on the group. Feelings of helplessness and hopelessness about the situation translated into decreased productivity and morale. What is not known are the effects on the physical health of group members, but they probably had more health concerns like colds, insomnia, digestive upsets, headaches, etc. The isolation and alienation from each other meant that each member considered him or herself to be the only one affected or that it would not be safe to talk about concerns with another group member. Thus, each member remained alone without the usual support they had previously experienced.

The illustration provides some idea of the distressing effects of a destructive narcissistic boss on a team. What follows are some suggestions for how to observe and understand a group with the idea that it is not easy to identify the gradual effects of destructive narcissism whether the person is a boss or a worker. Understanding the characteristics of a cohesive, productive group and what kinds of things to look for to determine the functioning of a group can provide indices of cohesiveness, lack of cohesiveness, and whether the group is experiencing the effects of a destructive narcissist.

What to Look For

Groups operate on more than one level: the immediate, observable level; the understood but more hidden level made up of the group norms or culture; and the unconscious level. The immediate, observable level can be perceived by members of the group and by external observers. These are the behaviors of group members and their verbal expressions.

The second level is not easily observed, as it is hidden. This is the level where the group's norms and culture develop. Norms and culture are the unspoken rules by which the group operates (decision-making, conflict and conflict resolution, inclusion/exclusion, etc.). Group members do not necessarily verbalize these operating rules but behave in accordance with them, and the rules are not readily apparent to an outside observer. However, if these behaviors are commented on or brought to the group's attention, members can readily agree on what's happening.

The third level is hidden from group members because it is composed of unconscious attitudes, needs, motivations, etc. Mostly it contains what individual members are not aware of about their "selves," but has considerable influence on both the individual and the group's functioning.

It's important to understand that all three levels combine to form the group, especially when trying to understand the impact of the destructive narcissistic worker. In addition to the impact on specific individuals, there is also a reaction from the group. What follows is a brief discussion of the levels for the group, and how these levels may be exhibited in behaviors and attitudes.

The Observable Level

All groups have an observable level of behaviors that can be commonly agreed upon by both group members and outside observers. While many inferences can be drawn about the meanings of these behaviors, some of which may be correct, no inferences are needed about what the behaviors are. The behaviors fall loosely into the following categories:

- level of participation,
- communication patterns among members,
- communication skills,
- nonverbal behaviors,

- feelings expression,

- avoidance techniques,

- decision-making processes, and

- conflict-resolution process.

If you want to begin to understand the group, increasing your awareness of how the group is behaving in each of these categories is the first step. No one category describes the presence of a destructive narcissist. You have to observe a cluster of behaviors over several categories, and all categories may not be involved. What follows is a description of behaviors that need your attention.

Level of Participation

It can be helpful to observe the degree to which members participate in the group to get a sense of the usual level of participation for each member. Observation can also tell you who is committed to the group, who participates in accomplishing the task and interacting with others, and who is being excluded or is engaging in self-exclusion from the group.

Some members may have a lot to say in the group but actually do very little, while others may say little but do a lot. Observing the degree to which members participate both verbally and nonverbally while working on the task provides clues to who may have destructive narcissistic characteristics.

As you observe, focus on who are the high participators, who seem to be low participators, and those who have changed their level of participation. Patterns of participation change for a reason and may signal difficulties. For example, a decrease in participation for many members may be caused by the impact of the destructive narcissist.

You will also want to observe how members, especially the quiet ones, are treated by other members. The group may collude on an unconscious level to exclude a member for a variety of reasons, and when members are excluded, they decrease their level of participation and commitment to the group. Other reasons for exclusion include gender, race or ethnic group, socioeconomic class, and other diversity issues.

High participation does not always mean greater influence. Indeed, some of the most influential group members talk very little, but when they do, others are prone to listen to them and to incorporate their ideas. Noticing the pattern of influence helps to tune in to the natural group leader.

The level of participation is also useful for understanding the amount of rivalry and competition between members. Does the level of participation for some members diminish when the boss is not present and increase when he or she is present? They may be competing for the boss's attention and approval. Or the rivalry may be a struggle to become the group leader. There is more than one explanation for what is happening, but the important thing is to maintain awareness, and you can do that through careful observation.

Communication Patterns

Note patterns of communication among group members. If two or more members seem to only talk to each other or seldom talk to other members, this can signal the development of a clique. Cliques or subgroups form because these members believe that they get more gratification from the relationship with each other than they receive from the entire group (Yalom 1995). This subgrouping usually begins with socializing outside the group (lunching together or stopping at a bar after work). It then moves to telephone or other outside-work communications, attending social events together, and visiting each other's homes. Sometimes the members will engage in business activities together or even become sexually involved. There are also times when the clique forms in the workplace and is confined there.

It should be remembered that this subgrouping occurs around perceived similarities and members can bond without being consciously aware that they are doing so. Some cliques form naturally without any conscious effort on anyone's part.

How do you identify the members of a clique or subgroup? These are the members who:

- generally agree with each other no matter what is being discussed,

- do not confront each other,

- may respond only to each other when in a meeting, and

- may make a point of arriving and leaving together.

Several cliques may signal the presence of a destructive narcissist in the group.

Communication Skills

Another factor to observe is the level of communication skill evidenced by each member. That is, to what extent they:

- use active listening, where both the content and the feeling are responded to;

- try to clarify terms, so as to make sure that what they heard was what was meant;

- use nonverbal attending skills such as facing the speaker, being quiet when others are speaking, maintaining eye contact, etc.;

- are distracted when interacting with others so that they give the impression that they are uninterested in the topic and the speaker;

- make pronouncements instead of talking with others;

- interrupt when others are talking; or

- display nonverbal signs of disinterest or contempt.

Use of effective communication skills play an important part in the productive functioning of the group. The presence of a destructive narcissist will have a significant effect on the effectiveness of communication in group.

Nonverbal Behaviors

Observation of nonverbal behaviors would include noticing behaviors that may indicate: status, boundary violations or defenses, and intimidation tactics. A brief example for each follows.

Status nonverbal behaviors include noticing:

- who initiates contact most frequently,

- who initiates touching, and

- deferential or contempt gestures.

Those who consider their status to be higher will usually initiate contact more frequently. For example, a boss usually initiates contact more frequently than do the workers. The exception to this is when initiating contact is a part of the job, such as for a secretary or administrative assistant. So, too, do those who perceive themselves as having higher status more frequently initiate touching. Touching can range from something like a tap on the shoulder to an actual hug. Gestures of deference are generally made to the individual considered to be of higher status. These include such behaviors such as:

- lowered head and/or eyes,

- becoming quiet when the person of higher status is speaking, or

- not giving input or disagreeing with the person, and

- performing service tasks for the person such as bringing them coffee or getting them needed materials.

Gestures of contempt include "looking down your nose" at someone. Looking down the nose can be seen when someone moves their head back and up, eyelids are lowered to cover part of the eye, and the neck becomes stiff. Other contemptuous gestures include failing to attend when the other person is speaking, having a sneer on the face when interacting with another person, and ignoring individuals.

Boundary violations are described in several chapters and do not need to be repeated here. What is useful to observe is who most often tends to engage in boundary violations, such as not knocking before entering someone's office. Becoming aware of the extent of boundary violations helps to identify the person or persons who feel this sense of entitlement.

Defenses against boundary violations are more difficult to observe but are also very useful in identifying the destructive narcissist as well as pointing out potential problem areas. Defenses, such as the following, are nonverbal indications of protection against boundary violations.

- Coworkers start to lock rooms, file cabinets, and desks where it was not previously done and the sensitivity of the material has not changed.

- There are closed doors where before doors were left open.

- People start firmly marking off personal space such as putting possessions on the table at a meeting that define their space.

Examples of *intimidation tactics* are found in voice tone and speech patterns, physical intrusion, and use of eye contact. People who talk loudly and rapidly are conveying hostility and an attempt to dominate. They come across to others as intimidating because:

- no one else can get a word in,

- they talk over and through others,

- they keep the attention on them by forcing others to listen intently because their speech is so rapid, and

- they can always raise their voice more loudly than anyone else.

This voice tone and pattern can be particularly intimidating to shy people, those who tend to be introverted and reflective, and to women and men who have reason to associate this way of speaking with physical or emotional abuse.

Physical intrusion is a boundary violation but is presented here as also being an intimidation tactic. Physical intrusion occurs when one person violates another person's sense of physical, personal space. They stand too close, sit too close for comfort, lean in too far, etc. They appear to deliberately use their body to make others feel uncomfortable. They may also do such things as:

- loom over the other person and look down on them, either when the other person is standing or sitting;

- lean into them and read over their shoulder;

- step closer than the usual comfort zone when talking to someone; or

- initiate unwanted touching.

Eye contact and use of the eyes can be very intimidating, especially when accompanied with some other facial expressions. Eye behaviors such as glaring, staring, and maintaining eye contact too long are examples of using the eyes to intimidate. Glaring is usually accompanied by other facial expressions, such as frowns or pursued lips, to express displeasure. This nonverbal behavior is intended to send a message to the other person and is designed to force them to deal with the displeasure in some way. Staring is very uncomfortable to the recipient. It can arouse a great deal of uncertainty and fear because the unblinking gaze conveys a sense of menace. Stares, by most people, are reserved for the unusual, and when someone is the target of a stare they often feel that the other person sees something wrong, etc. Too, in the animal world and in some parts of the human world, a stare is used to transfix or paralyze prey so that it will not run away when attacked. All of these are some reasons why a stare can be intimidating. The final example of using eyes to intimidate is by holding eye contact too long. Sustained eye contact conveys interest and, in the case of lovers, intimacy. However, when the real relationship is one that does not include intimacy or the desire for intimacy, sustained eye contact can become discomforting and intimidating.

Feeling Expression

Observation of feelings expression include noting if:

- feelings are expressed openly and appropriately;

- feelings, especially uncomfortable ones, are suppressed;

- there is an increase of inappropriate expressions of feelings; and

- there is an increase of complaints about having uncomfortable feelings.

This set of behaviors can also be primary clues to the presence of a destructive narcissist in a unit. The behavior and attitudes of a destructive narcissist produce or trigger anger, frustration, fear, dread, loathing, and other uncomfortable feelings in individuals. These feelings also spill over and have an impact on the workplace environment and outside personal relationships, as well as collectively impacting the entire unit.

Some variation of the following is likely to happen when feelings aroused by the destructive narcissist spill over to the entire unit. Members develop a lower tolerance for frustration and differences of opinion. Even when members try to make a conscious effort not to let their personal feelings get displaced onto others, there is some seepage, and quirks that were previously tolerated become irksome. Members seem cranky, apologize more often to each other for what they say and how they say it, and the expression of positive feelings is significantly decreased. In other words, members begin to displace the negative feelings aroused by the destructive narcissist on their coworkers, producing feelings of uncertainty, wariness, and cautiousness in practically everyone. Attacks, both direct and indirect, increase and become more common, and considerable effort is expended by individuals to prevent being attacked, defending against attacks, and in retaliation. Members who continue to try and interact with each other find that they are either fighting or fleeing.

In extreme instances, members may even engage in shouting matches, or arguments with name-calling or resort to physical fights. This completes the demoralization of the unit. Feelings are certainly being openly expressed, but their expression is not appropriate.

Avoidance Techniques

A dead giveaway that there is a destructive narcissist in the unit is the use of avoidance techniques by workers. If the destructive narcissist is the boss, the avoidance techniques will likely be more subtle than when the destructive narcissist is a coworker. However, in both instances avoidance will not be blatant, as most people will begin to use these techniques without conscious awareness.

Avoidance techniques are designed to keep the person from encountering the destructive narcissist and having to experience the effects of their behaviors and attitudes, such as when they blame, criticize, distort, and lie. The unpredictability (or predictability) of having the destructive narcissist do or say something that leads to frustration, anger, or feelings of incompetence promotes the desire to avoid interactions with them as much as possible. The distressing outcome or effect when avoidance techniques are used by many or most of the unit is that they also begin to avoid each other. Isolation and feelings of alienation increase, contributing to decreased morale and productivity. The description of the effects of a destructive narcissist on a unit illustrates many common avoidance techniques.

Decision-Making

Observe how the unit makes decisions. Which of the following is most often used:

- appeals to authority,

- someone taking the authority to make decisions for the group,

- majority rule,

- decisions made by a few and others forced or manipulated into agreement, or

- obtaining consensus?

Other questions to consider are whether there is someone who tries to impose their decision on the group and if all members are included in the deliberations where everyone has input into the decision.

It's especially important to become aware of any shifts in how the group arrives at decisions. For example, where once consensus was the preferred method for decision-making, the group now wants to vote on practically everything, and dissenting opinions or differing points of view are given little hearing or credence. Something caused the shift, and whatever it was, the group has decided that the best way to get the job done is to stifle dissent and to operate within more rigid parameters.

If the group uses decision-making by appeals to authority, particularly if this is a shift in behavior, members are not feeling confident about the quality of decisions made and/or their decisions are being overturned or overruled on a regular basis. The group is not sure how to proceed and are resorting to asking the authority figure what to do.

Another way of making decisions is when one person in the group becomes the "self-authorized" decision maker for the group, and the group allows this to happen. The self-authorized decision maker does not ask for nor tolerate input from others. This person assumes that they are the most qualified or in the best position to make a decision and feels no need to include other group members in the decision-making process. They impose their decisions on the group.

In an effort to stifle dissent some groups may use the "majority rule." That is, that the idea or proposal with the most votes becomes the decision for the group. So, the person who has the most influence or is the best manipulator is the one whose ideas are most likely to win, regardless of the merit of the idea. Having winners and losers in the unit is not conducive to good morale.

If there is a clique or subgroup in the unit, decisions may be made by them and forced on the group or other members manipulated into agreement. Their solidarity provides strength and impetus for their proposed decisions, and because other members are not united, they may find it difficult or impossible to counteract. However, those who are not included in the decision-making process do begin to resent being excluded.

Decision-making by consensus means that the process has included input from all members, and efforts were made to consider all viewpoints before reaching a decision. When decisions are made by consensus, all members are included, their viewpoints respected, and the group does not have winners and losers. Because all members are a part of the process there is greater commitment to carrying out the decision.

Conflict-Resolution Process

How does the group handle conflict among members?

- Is conflict ignored or suppressed?

- Do members isolate themselves to minimize the possibility of conflict emerging?

- Has conflict and disagreement among members increased?

- Do members appear irritable, touchy, and easily angered?

These behaviors and attitudes may signal the impact of a destructive narcissist on the unit, and some of the feelings aroused by this person may be displaced on coworkers.

Trying to pretend that conflict does not exist by ignoring, suppressing, or withdrawing can work for a short time. Some conflicts may even dissipate if left alone, but few fall into this category. Pretending that a conflict does not exist is generally not an effective approach to conflict resolution. The feelings are driven underground where they can fester and negatively impact relationships in indirect ways.

When group members choose isolation as their conflict-resolution strategy, the entire group suffers because interactions are decreased, the climate for subgrouping to occur is enhanced, and members begin to feel excluded from the real work of the group—

even though they chose to exclude themselves. Retreating from the fray certainly reduces the possibility of conflict, but it also reduces the likelihood that the group will become cohesive and productive.

One outcome of having a destructive narcissist in the group is increased friction among members. This result is because of manipulation by this person and/or because feelings triggered by this person get displaced on other group members. The group uses fighting, attacks, and intimidation as conflict-resolution strategies, and the group then becomes an unsafe environment with members constantly at each other's throats or defending against an attack. Morale and productivity suffer.

Cues to the Hidden Levels

The previous discussion focused on observable behaviors that can be subjected to an objective appraisal. There is also a non-observable level where inferences can be made, but the inferences may not be objective and, for this reason, may not be verifiable or correct. On the other hand, this level is very important in understanding the impact of the destructive narcissist on the unit as it incorporates feelings, hidden agendas, and nonconscious attitudes, as well as presence or absence of some behaviors designed to promote the emotional well-being of the group.

Group Atmosphere

Groups have an atmosphere that can be best described as a general impression of how the group works. For example, a group could be described as friendly and congenial, as disagreeable and conflict-ridden, or as professional and focused. Each of these descriptors suggests ways in which the group accomplishes its task and members relate to each other. When trying to determine if a destructive narcissist is present, it can be helpful to reflect on the group's atmosphere and try to characterize it with one or two descriptive words that give an impression of how the group works.

There are a group of behaviors that are designed to further the work of the group by promoting teamwork and an atmosphere that capitalizes on the expertise of each group member. When these behaviors are present, the group generally works well together and members feel positive about the group. When these behaviors are absent, teamwork is also absent, and members do not feel positive about the group. The primary behaviors that fall into this category are:

- encouraging and praising,

- trying to promote harmony among members,
- suggesting compromises so that there are not winners and losers, and
- doing and saying things that help the group stay aware of its norms.

The presence of a destructive narcissist most often means a reduction or elimination of these behaviors.

Hidden Agendas

Where there are secret, underlying motives for what is done or said, a hidden agenda exists. Hidden agendas are very detrimental to a group's morale and productivity, especially when the hidden agendas have one or more of the following motives: to manipulate, to gain power or control, or to undermine others. They destroy trust and feelings of safety, leading to a decrease in effective working relationships which, in turn, negatively impact productivity. Understanding how a destructive narcissist operates points out the importance of the impact of hidden agendas on the workplace.

Masking Feelings

Group members may begin to mask feelings instead of openly expressing them or may express them in inappropriate ways. These are some nonconscious ways of responding to the destructive narcissist and may be difficult to directly observe. Masking feelings is done when people feel that it is not to their advantage to openly express their emotions.

One indirect way of noting that feelings are being withheld or masked is through the increase of physical problems in the group, such as ulcers, high blood pressure, heart disease, frequent colds and flu, etc. There may also be higher incidences of stress-related psychological problems, such as depression and addiction. Members may also report more relationship problems with family and friends. The consequences of masking feelings are far reaching, affecting lives in numerous ways.

Summary

The effects and impact of a destructive narcissist in the workplace are significant and important to productivity and morale. Because their behaviors and attitudes are not easily or often identified as such, the effects are attributed to other things such as competition, personality clashes, bad attitudes, and laziness. Individuals become alienated and isolated, leading to less and less cohesiveness.

Chapter 9

Interactions and Relationships

When You Cannot Avoid Interacting

It's likely that you will not be able to sever all interactions and relations with the boss or coworker who has a destructive narcissistic pattern. Without help, you will also probably not be able to prevent these interactions from:

- leaving you with many unpleasant feelings,

- eroding your self-confidence and self-esteem, and

- causing you to act out of character and/or displace anger and aggression on others.

Even if you are able to repress or deny the person's impact on you, that impact will manifest itself in other ways. One of the most negative outcomes could be health-related ailments, such as headaches, increased blood pressure, reduced immunity to colds and flu, or other conditions. In short, you can experience significant negative psychological and physical impacts on your person. This chapter explains, in part, what can happen during interactions with destructive narcissists and why they can have such a significant impact on the psychological and physical well-being of others. I'll also provide some strategies for preventing, moderating, and eliminating the impact this person has on you. The primary assumptions underlying these suggestions are that you cannot change the person or the situation, so you have to work with your personal resources.

Frustrating Behaviors

The quality of your interactions with someone who has a destructive narcissistic pattern is probably very low. You may leave many such interactions feeling very angry, confused, or frustrated, and sometimes feeling all of these and more. Over time you may begin to doubt yourself. After all, others appear to be able to handle their interactions with this person, so you may begin to feel that you are somehow at fault.

Some common complaints from people who interact with destructive narcissists are that they:

- attack you without provocation or cause;
- give erroneous information but claim that you misunderstood or are wrong;
- constantly lie, distort, and mislead;
- cannot see other perspectives;
- do not understand what others are feeling;
- are very adept at blaming and criticizing;
- make devaluing statements to the person's face;
- always, or almost always, have something negative to say about almost everyone;
- are very admiring of superiors;
- brag about their possessions, accomplishments, etc., and are disparaging of others';
- can shift the focus of every discussion to themselves; and
- believe they are never, ever wrong.

These complaints are serious enough by themselves but added to these is the uncertainty about what to expect during the interaction. You will find that you probably tend to approach an interaction based on your previous experiences with the person, and feel prepared to deal with that, only to find that they do something different that is just as disruptive. For example, if in a previous interaction the destructive narcissist lied to you or gave you misleading information, you may approach the current interaction expecting that they will attempt to lie or mislead. You are prepared to challenge them, ask for verification, or have enough facts to let them know that you are aware that they are lying and that you suspect that it is deliberate on their part. However, what you encounter is not another lie but an unexpected attack. The destructive narcissist immediately goes on the offensive and attacks you, blaming you for something you did not do. You are once again caught off guard and end up with many of the same unpleasant feelings you had in the previous interaction.

Double Bind

Destructive narcissists can also be very adept at putting you in a double bind. They will make accusations or ask questions that seem to defy simply answers or explanations. A personal example can illustrate this. I was once told by a destructive narcissistic boss to stop doing something that I did not do and was not doing. My response was that I did not do what she accused me of doing, and her response was "Just stop it." How can you stop doing something you were not doing in the first place?

Switching Topics

These people can also be very adept at switching topics in midconversation. You begin discussing one topic, and somewhere along the line you realize that they are talking about something else. If you point this out to them, their response is usually that you're being stupid, that you're unable to perceive a simple connection, or that they did not change the topic, you did. Considerable confusion can result from this switcheroo, and it is even worse when you only realize in retrospect that the topic was changed.

Another way they can pull a switch on you is to shift the focus from the original topic to them. All of a sudden you realize that the emphasis is on them and not the subject you wanted to discuss. Usually we are too polite to point out to them that they shifted the topic to a personal focus. We can point out a topic shift and refocus the discussion when it is a cognitive or objective topic, but are less likely or able to do so when the shift is on a personal level. It can be difficult for us to try to refocus on the original topic because we do not want to appear insensitive or uncaring. We tend to lose either way, whether we call the shift to their attention or ignore it.

Relationships

Take some time and evaluate the quality of your relationship with the person you've identified as having a destructive narcissistic pattern. As you reflect on the following relationship components, also keep in mind that you cannot change that person. You can only adapt *your* behaviors, attitudes, and feelings. Try not to indulge in thoughts like, "if only they would," or "if I change this way they will change that way." They are very unlikely to change, see no need to do so, and are unaffected by anything you say or do.

Below I've listed some components of a healthy and mutually beneficial relationship. These are not all of the elements that comprise good relationships but may be some of the most significant ones in the workplace.

- Mutual respect
- Projections
- Warmth and positive regard
- Honesty and genuineness
- A spirit of cooperation

Mutual Respect

Respect for others means that they are valued as worthwhile, unique individuals and not considered to be extensions of self. Some destructive narcissists can be thought of as not having completely separated and individuated from his or her parent or primary nurturer. They did not fully complete this developmental phase and continue to perceive and behave toward others in ways that indicate that they do not consider others to be fully differentiated from them. When one has achieved sufficient differentiation, it manifests itself in such things as appreciation of others and recognition of their space, territory, and possessions. In other words, respect for both the physical and psychological boundaries. Boundaries are discussed in chapters 2 through 7.

Projections

Projection works like this: there is a part of self or a characteristic that is feared, disliked, or unwanted. In order to get rid of it and not accept that the self contains it, the feared part is "projected" on a target person, and the target can then be rejected, disrespected, or disliked for having that characteristic. For example, if someone fears or dislikes their own anger, they may project it on someone else and describe or react to the other person as if they are angry. Destructive narcissists have many characteristics they find, on an unconscious level, to be unacceptable. They often get rid of these "faults" by projection. So when they show a lack of respect to you or someone else, it could be that they do not objectively perceive you or the other person as you are but are reacting to you in terms of their own projections. When you are the target of a projection you are often left with confusion and/or anger after an interaction with the projector. There may be other reasons for your feelings, but if you leave an interaction with the distinct perception that the other person did not respect you, then you may have been the target of their projections. Workplace relationships can be difficult when there are many targets.

Projection is a defense mechanism that is probably used by almost everyone at some time. Destructive narcissists can have very intense and powerful projections to defend themselves against feared destruction or abandonment. In contrast, people who have fewer and less deep levels of underdeveloped narcissism engage in less projection because they have less need to defend their "self." Destructive narcissists act on their projections by disliking or rejecting the targets of the projections because the targets are being perceived as having the disliked or disowned part of the destructive narcissist, while the more developed person is able to more objectively perceive others. There are some reasons why it is important to have an awareness of your projections.

Warmth and Positive Regard

Satisfactory work relationships are also characterized by warmth and positive regard. While the characteristics differ in intensity and kind from those in your more intimate relationships, the quality of work relationships is enhanced when you feel good about your coworkers.

How are these characteristics manifested? You tend to perceive and react to others in terms of your essential character and the extent to which you have had positive and negative relationships with others. For example, if you have been betrayed frequently by others whom you trusted, you might tend to be somewhat wary and tentative in accepting or establishing relationships. You were hurt and do not want to be hurt again, so your behavior may be somewhat cool and distant. You may want to get closer to others but fear you may be betrayed again.

Your inner self is important, but your observable behavior is also important. What others see you doing and saying plays a part in how they perceive you as having warmth and positive regard toward them. Observable behaviors, such as the following, convey warmth.

- Eye contact
- Body oriented toward the speaker
- Relaxed arms and hands position
- Slight forward lean
- Smiles and other attending behaviors

Openness to listening to others, valuing their opinions and ideas, and willingness to accept personal responsibility are other ways of showing positive regard.

Destructive narcissists can exhibit many of these behaviors, but they do not have the inner resources to sustain them for any length of time. Therefore, it is through a series of interactions over time that one begins to understand that destructive narcissists are not warm and caring but rather distant and uncaring. They can be very attentive to someone at the beginning of the relationship, but when they perceive that that person is not reflecting their inflated self-opinion and/or cannot be of use or service to them, then they cease being attentive. This is one reason why it takes so long for you to realize what is happening in the relationship.

Honesty and Genuineness

Satisfying relationships are built on mutual trust. It's difficult to feel that any relationship is fulfilling if you cannot trust the other person. You have to be able to rely on the person's honesty, truthfulness, and genuineness in order to trust that they have your best interests at heart and will not knowingly mislead you.

Destructive narcissists can knowingly lie and mislead in order to further their own agenda. They cannot be honest in their self-appraisal as so much of who they are is walled off and is unconscious. They cannot see themselves as they are or as others see them. Indeed, they will make every effort to only associate with those who can admire and flatter them. They seek to be envied and powerful and assume that everyone else has the same needs and desires. This is one of the reasons why they will ascribe deception and malicious motives to others. Those are their motives, and they feel that everyone else also has them as guiding principles. Being any other way is foreign and not understandable to them.

Again, it may only be through interactions over a period of time that you begin to realize that someone is not honest, truthful, or genuine in their relationship with you. Expecting destructive narcissists to be any other way is unrealistic, and if you were to confront them with their behavior, they would dismiss it as an attempt on your part to undermine them. They will say and do whatever they feel is important to gain what they want or feel is their due.

A Spirit of Cooperation

Satisfying relationships in the work setting will have a spirit of cooperation. There will be:

- sharing of ideas and resources,
- support for each other,
- a willingness to assume responsibility and share information,
- a willingness to share recognition for the work done,
- little or no criticizing of each other,
- no attempts to off-load blame,
- no devaluing or disparaging remarks made about each other, and
- no attempts to form cliques or coalitions against anyone.

There may be some competition, but it's the kind of competition that is energizing and not depressive. This kind of competition does not arouse aggression to the point that it is destructive but acts as more of an encouragement to everyone to put forth their best effort. This kind of competition also recognizes that the best effort is through cooperation and teamwork and not only through individual effort.

Destructive narcissists do not trust others enough to really be a part of a team. They will undermine all efforts unless they are guaranteed that others will do the work and they will receive the credit. This does not mean that they do not do anything. They may do some part of the work, but:

- do not assume their fair share,
- perform their jobs poorly,
- blame others for their mistakes, and
- what is most distressing, take credit for the positive outcomes.

Destructive narcissists make sure their names are on everything submitted. There is a Dilbert cartoon where Dogbert notes that it is easier to take credit for others' work than it is for you to do any work. Four examples are given for how you can take unearned credit:

- tell someone you agree with what they are saying and ask that they put you on as coauthor,

- tell the author of a report that you will give it to the boss while planning to suggest to the boss that you really wrote it,

- put a cover page to the report with you name on it, or

- hear someone express an idea and then present the idea to the boss as if it were yours.

There are many other ways to take unearned credit. Another way is when you are asked for ideas or there are brainstorming sessions and someone volunteers to write up the suggestions. You don't find out until sometime later that the report only has the name of the person who wrote the suggestions and not names of others who provided ideas. The volunteer writer may even have a statement that others contributed but never names them, and so the boss or other readers only have that one name. This person then receives the credit. They usually also make sure that their name is in fairly large or bold letters.

Personal Resources

In this chapter I've tried to offer some of the behaviors you might experience from a destructive narcissist. These are but a few of the behaviors and attitudes. You must remain aware that it usually takes time for you to realize what they are doing. The impact of their behaviors and attitudes is immediately felt, but most of us tend to ignore or rationalize it and are at first unable or unwilling to recognize the destructiveness of the interactions we have with these people.

Many people are not usually in a position where they can effectively challenge destructive narcissists, insist that they change, or walk away from the job. There are times when having to interact and work with this person is very depressing and can make you feel impotent and helpless. These feelings do not go away or moderate as time goes on. They tend to increase and intensify, thereby having a negative impact on your health, psychological well-being, and other relationships. Some of their behaviors, such as blaming and criticizing, can begin to erode our self-confidence and self-esteem, especially when the boss fails to recognize or accept what they are doing and appears to buy in to their perspective or opinion.

However bad the situation may be, however helpless and powerless you may feel, all is not lost. There are actions you can take to make your situation more palatable, increase your ability to effectively manage the impact of the destructive narcissist on you, and make your work experience more positive.

In addition to actions, there are some attitude shifts that can be helpful. The most important and critical one is that you can only work with *your* personal resources, you cannot change the other person. No matter how cordial, understanding, appreciative, admiring, caring, or accommodating you are, they will not see the error of their ways and change their behavior. Also, you cannot force them to change. No amount of rejection, threats, arguments, confrontation, etc., will bring about change. Until you can accept your relative powerlessness to change this person, you will continue to be frustrated in your interactions and in the relationship.

The following discussion presents some suggestions for actions and attitude shifts that can make a positive difference for you. Chapters 2 and 5 also present suggested actions to effectively cope with a colleague or boss who has many of the destructive narcissist's behaviors and attitudes. As you read these suggestions, try and think of how you can implement them and modify them to fit your situation and your personality.

Your Strengths

One of the most positive steps you can take is to conduct an inventory of your personal strengths. This action helps to focus your energy and thoughts in positive ways and is much more constructive than continuing to berate yourself for not being more effective or to fret and fume because the destructive narcissist is the way they are. An inventory will help you mobilize your strongest personal resources to better deal with this person.

The following exercise is one way of taking an inventory.

Exercise 9-1: Focus on Strengths

Materials: Sheet of paper, pens or pencil, ruler, and a place where you can write undisturbed for twenty to thirty minutes.

1. Begin the exercise by drawing a line down the center of the page and labeling the two columns as follows:

Accomplishments and Continuing Personal Characteristics

2. The next step is to number 1 through 10 along the left side of the page, leaving about two inches for writing between each number.

3. List ten lifetime accomplishments in the column labeled "Accomplishments." You should list items that carry some measure of personal pride for you. They do not have to be heroic accomplishments, just those that are significant for you. You can use childhood accomplishments, but try to have four to five from your adult life. They do not all have to be work related—personal and family achievements can also be listed.

4. Considering each accomplishment separately, try to remember what it felt like when you were in that period of your life and in the particular situation. Next, focus on what personal strengths or characteristics allowed or helped you to accomplish the task or goal. Other people may have contributed to the accomplishment, but the focus for this exercise is you. Write all the strengths you can think of for each accomplishment in the second column. Repeat strengths if they contribute to more than one accomplishment.

5. When the two lists are complete, read over what you wrote and allow yourself to feel proud again. These are the personal resources that can help you effectively manage interactions and relationships with the destructive narcissist.

Capitalizing on Your Strengths

After you identify your strengths you can begin to capitalize on them. It may take some thought and effort to understand how and when to use them, but the results will be worth your time.

For example, suppose you identify the following as some strengths that appear in several of your accomplishments:

- determination,
- reliability,
- assertiveness,
- perseverance,
- oriented toward goals,
- can easily shift attention when needed.

These strengths can be used when interacting with the destructive narcissist in many ways. You could reaffirm your determination that you will not let that person get next to you and trigger unpleasant emotions. You could highlight your reliability in getting tasks done and increase your willingness to let others know that they can depend on you. Assertiveness is a major asset when dealing with destructive narcissists, as it will enable you to not become overpowered by their demands and find yourself doing what they want you to do instead of what you want to do. Persistence is a trait that allows you to continue in the face of adversity. Dealing with destructive narcissists is certainly adversity and persisting in maintaining your boundaries could be a strategy. As you can see from these examples, there are many ways to use your strengths.

Your Unrecognized Strengths

You probably also have some unrecognized strengths. Most everyone has some, but they usually remain hidden and underused. Some of these strengths can be identified through a review of what you consider to be weaknesses or for which you are criticized. To identify these potential strengths make a list of all personal characteristics you consider deficits or weaknesses. Add to the list any traits for which others criticize you, even if you do not agree with the criticism. Taking each item separately, try to identify at least one strength for it. Following are some examples of criticisms and the strengths related to them.

Criticism	Strength
Abrupt manner	Stays focused on essentials, does not need details, uses time well
Cries easily	Very empathic, sensitive to others, open, emotionally expressive
Impulsive	Spontaneous, able to quickly see patterns and potentials, decisive
Withdrawn	Reflective, uses inner resources, tolerates isolation

Self-Esteem

Your self-esteem can be a valuable resource even though it may take a beating from having to interact and relate with a destructive narcissist. By "self-esteem" I mean the degree of confidence and satisfaction you have with yourself. This is different from your self-concept. Self-concept is considered to be the mental image you have of yourself. Self-esteem is more concerned with feelings about oneself, although these feelings can contribute to the image one has of oneself.

Your self-esteem can be eroded and undermined when constantly bombarded with criticisms, blame, and disparaging and devaluing remarks. Even when your self-confidence and self-satisfaction are high, you can suffer some erosion because you are open to self-examination. Destructive narcissists do not face this erosion because they are closed to any self-examination and do not see that there is any need for them to change in any way. If you are the type of person who is somewhat introspective and willing to look at who you are, reflecting on your behavior and its impact on others, you are more likely to experience some erosion of your self-esteem as a result of your interactions with destructive narcissists.

To bolster your self-esteem and halt and/or prevent additional erosion you can do some of the following. Many are internal states and you do not have to talk about them to anyone.

- Focus on your accomplishments, not disappointments.
- Pay attention to signs of physical stress and take immediate steps to manage the stress.
- Strengthen your personal relationships with family and friends.
- Compliment yourself.
- Expand your creativity in something that is enjoyable to you.
- Try a new activity that involves creating.
- Find someone you trust and "vent" without expecting them to solve the problem.
- Restore or remind yourself of your meaning in life, your goals, and your aspirations.
- Reaffirm your strengths on a daily basis.
- Put some delights in your life. These are the little things that give us pleasure.
- Laugh.

Insulation

You may need to institute some emotional insulation between you and destructive narcissists to prevent your more intense unpleasant emotions from emerging. One of the reasons these people are so difficult to deal with is that they have an uncanny knack for triggering your feelings, especially those that you consider destructive or uncomfortable, such as anger.

There are two major reasons why these feelings get triggered: personal issues or unfinished business and what mental health professionals term as "projective identification." Personal concerns or unfinished business are likely to be the most significant reason why you experience these unpleasant emotions with destructive narcissists, and their importance should not be underestimated. However, these are concerns that are best dealt with in therapy or through self-exploration and are beyond the scope of this book.

The other reason, projective identification, is also important and may explain why you are puzzled about some of the emotions you experience or about their intensity. I explained projection earlier as taking an unwanted part of self and putting it on the other person and then acting toward them as if they had the unwanted part. "Projective identification" begins with the projection, but the other person then takes the projection in and identifies with all or part of it and is further manipulated to act out the projection. Projective identification is much more complicated and involved than projection.

In order for a projective identification to occur:

- the projector must have powerful projections,

- the receiver must have some susceptibility to receiving and incorporating projections, perhaps personal issues that cause him or her to identify with all or part of the projections, and

- the projector must be able to manipulate the receiver to act out or on the projection.

All of this battle takes place on an unconscious level. Neither party is consciously participating.

An example of a projective identification occurs when you are in an interaction and become angry or afraid. You are aware that you are angry but may be confused as to why you are angry or why you are so intensely angry. Your conscious mind is telling you that it's not reasonable or necessary to be this angry, but you seem helpless to do anything about it. What may be happening is that the other person was angry but feared their anger and wanted to disown it. They then projected the disowned anger on you. You received their anger, added it to your already existing irritation, identified with the angry feelings, and then acted on those feelings by becoming even more angry. You may even have experienced some body tension like clenched fists and jaws, used angry words and tone of voice, or even became somewhat violent (like smashing your fist on the table). As you were doing and experiencing all this, you were asking yourself, "What the . . . is going on?"

Destructive narcissists have powerful, primitive feelings and tend to be powerful projectors of these feelings. The primitive feelings of rage and fear dominate them, and since these are uncomfortable feelings, they seek to get rid of them as much as possible. Reflect on the interactions you've had with someone you consider a destructive narcissistic. Have you ever walked away feeling very angry and churned up while they were perfectly fine, even though they were the one who was on the "hot seat"? It could be that they got rid of their feelings by projecting them on you and causing you to act on them—leaving you with all the anger.

If the reason that you experience unpleasant feelings after encountering the person is projective identification there is a two-pronged approach that can help. The first is to understand and work through any personal issues that may cause you to take in projections and identify with all or part of them. This is best accomplished with the guidance and support of a therapist and cannot be addressed in this book. The second is an immediate "Band-Aid" to help protect you at this point. It can enable you to better tolerate interactions with destructive narcissists so that you do not have to constantly experience these unpleasant emotions.

The second approach is called "insulation," and you have to select your own method for initiating it. What follows is a description of the method I use. When I anticipate or know that I must interact with a person I have reason to believe is a destructive narcissist, I consciously prepare by visualizing massive steel doors shut tightly between us. The visualization includes the process of shutting and locking the doors. There is also a clang as they close. Once I started using this method for emotional insulation, I was no longer troubled with projections and projective identification. I could accept and work through my feelings with more assurance that they were indeed mine and not those from the other person. The emotions I experienced were milder and more easily managed. The downside was that I felt more alienated and remote, which was not how I want to be generally. But I knew that if I tried to reach out to this person as I do with most people I would only be opening myself up to their projections and projective identifications.

You will need to develop your own visualizations for insulating yourself. Use whatever seems appropriate to you to block off the projections and projective identifications. You will continue to experience some discomfort at times, but this will happen less and less often. What is important to remember is that you need to consciously use your visualization every time you know you will have to interact with that person. Insulating yourself has to become a habit.

What can be disconcerting is when you cannot anticipate an interaction. It will take some practice to learn that you need to quickly visualize your insulation when you unexpectedly run into the person. "Ever vigilant" is a motto to keep in mind.

Cognitive Techniques

There are several cognitive techniques that can be of assistance:

- thought stopping,
- analyzing,
- distracting,
- refocusing, and
- relaxation.

These are called "cognitive" because you will have to consciously think instead of just reacting on a feeling level. The feelings will still be there and still be important, but you will be able to better manage them because you are exercising conscious control.

Thought Stopping

Thought stopping can assist when you find yourself in the downward spiral of self-blame, depression, or fantasizing "getting rid of" the person. Once you embark on any of these you will find that your negative feelings tend to intensify. Interrupt the downward movement by consciously deciding to stop. You do not have to continue thinking about whatever is distressing you—you can decide not to. It does not matter if you are somewhat unsuccessful at first and keep returning to the distress. This may very well happen. What does matter is that every time you find yourself back in the thought pattern that you once again decide to stop. Keep trying, and you will find that you can do it.

Analyzing

Analyzing is also a cognitive technique that requires conscious thought. Mentally take a step back and try to understand what the other person is doing or really means, what your response is, and why you are having this response. In other words, you try to objectively observe what is occurring between you and the other person, what their real meanings are, and why you are reacting the way you do. Once you begin to analyze, you will find that the feelings moderate and there are times when some real understanding and insight can take place.

Use some of the material presented in preceding chapters for your analysis. For example, you could check out if your boundary was violated and understand that you are angry because of that violation. Further, you may begin to understand that you are also upset that you allowed the person to violate your boundary without saying or doing anything about it. You could explore the source of your anger and begin to understand it better. You could also remind yourself that you do not have to accept the violation and that there are steps you can take to reduce or eliminate it. Realizing that you do have some control and power will help moderate your negative feelings about the person's behavior.

Distracting

Another technique is to distract yourself from whatever you're thinking and feeling. This is a way of interrupting whatever is distressing. When you interrupt you give yourself an opportunity to reflect and soothe your upset.

To distract yourself, consciously think of something else. You may need to plan how to distract yourself so that when you find yourself in a situation where you want to use distraction, you will not flounder or be unable to distract yourself. Plan to think of something pleasant or just something different. For example, when you find yourself in an interaction with the destructive narcissist and realize that you are becoming upset, you could distract yourself from these feelings by imagining the person in an undignified position. For instance, you could suppose that they were standing on their heads while they talked to you or that they were leaning on a grocery cart full of ice cream that was melting. Anything silly or undignified would work.

Refocusing

Refocus your thoughts or the conversation. Just announce that you want to change the topic, or select some piece of the conversation and focus on that. Anything to gain control of the conversation and of your feelings. Do not accept that you have to follow their lead and talk about what they want to talk about.

For example, if the person is bringing up something in order to blame you or criticize you in some way, you could say that you will get back to that at some point. You can also add that you have been meaning to talk with them about something else and proceed to the new subject. Or you could say that what he or she brings up reminds you of something that they need to know or for which their input is needed. As you practice refocusing, you will become more adept at changing the topic.

Relaxing

When you find yourself having to deal with intense and unpleasant feelings you'll probably find it enormously helpful to consciously relax yourself. You will find that you are better able to handle any emotion when you are relaxed and can prevent them from intensifying or overwhelming you.

In order to relax, you have to consciously concentrate on your breathing and make it become deep and even. When you are under the influence of intense emotion you will find that your breathing tends to be shallow, comes only from the top of your lungs, and is very rapid. This leads to oxygen deprivation and can help to intensify negative feelings.

You will also have to attend to the tension in your muscles and body. Once you are aware of just where the tension is and how tight your muscles are, you will need to consciously let go of the tension. This can be accomplished by isolating muscle groups, tightening them and then relaxing them. You may want to buy a relaxation tape to practice with or take a class. You will be surprised at how much relaxation can put you back in control of what you are feeling.

Other Defenses

There are other defenses that may help such as ending the conversation, never being alone with the person, refusing to talk with them, and other avoidance strategies. These will protect you but do nothing to develop a working relationship that will enable you to be perceived as cooperative.

Remember to Avoid . . .

Coping strategies also involve not engaging in some behaviors. The following list are some behaviors that can lead to even more distress and disruption for you. They are counterproductive for both your job relations and for you personally. Further, some of these behaviors provide the destructive narcissist with additional ammunition to use against you. As you read through the list you may find that there are some behaviors you do display and some are foreign to you. Your task then is to guard against all of them, for if you have to interact constantly with destructive narcissists, you will probably find yourself engaging in uncharacteristic behaviors and attitudes.

Do not:

- confront,

- attack,

- whine and complain,

- assume that their superiors perceive them as you do,

- try to empathize,

- expect them to see the "error of their ways,"

- expect them to understand or care about your perspective,

- take what they say and do personally, even if they are mounting an offensive against you, or

- seek to form a coalition against them.

Summary

You can be effective in moderating the negative effects of the behaviors and attitudes of the destructive narcissist on you. This can be accomplished when you understand your personal responses better and when you institute some modest behavior and attitude changes of your own. This chapter is a good starting point for beginning to understand and change. Self-knowledge and the desire to change are the keys, along with an acceptance that you cannot change the other person.

Chapter 10

Managing Your Unpleasant Feelings

Personal Feelings and Reactions

Interactions with destructive narcissists are characterized by your experiencing some intense uncomfortable feelings that can be difficult to manage. That is, these feelings are not easily prevented or overcome. Almost every interaction can leave you with some unpleasant feelings, and it can seem that these exchanges are impossible to avoid. If you try and explain what happens during an interaction to others who do not know or interact with the destructive narcissist, they usually don't understand why you are reacting so negatively and intensely. When you try to objectively reflect on what occurred, even you may not understand your reactions. You just know that you are left with intense unpleasant feelings that are not easily dissipated.

You probably consider yourself a reasonable person who wants to try and get along with others, and so you may extend or increase your efforts to understand the destructive narcissist and to be congenial, only to find that you are still frequently experiencing unpleasant feelings. If you tend to be introspective and engage in self-examination you will use those techniques to try and understand what you're doing that causes these bad feelings. You may even blame yourself for not being "good enough" to meet the other person's expectations.

A recurring question you may ask yourself is some variation of "Why are they doing this?" and "Why does it bother me?" Neither can be answered without an understanding of how psychological growth and development occurs. What is most troubling, however, is that you may continue to obsess over these questions and not obtain answers that seem reasonable and understandable to you.

Of more immediate concern may be distress over how easily some of your unpleasant emotions can be triggered and how long they can linger. It probably seems that the harder you try to get along with the destructive narcissist, or no matter how much you try to manage your feelings, the more distress and self-doubt emerges. A considerable amount of your time and energy will be spent thinking about this unsatisfying relationship.

Previous chapters presented coping strategies you can employ that are associated with attitudes and behaviors of destructive narcissists. This chapter will focus on your responses to interactions and other relationship issues. After all, you do not want to continue to experience these emotions, nor do you want them to be so intense.

In the first part of the chapter I'll describe common emotions that can be triggered in interactions with destructive narcissists. These emotions can be troubling to you because they are not characteristic of your usual responses, nor do you understand why they are triggered. The other part of the presentation focuses on techniques and strategies you can use to better manage and dissipate the unpleasant emotions.

Categories, Levels, and Costs of Emotions

The categories of negative emotions you'll be dealing with when interacting with a destructive narcissist are guilt, shame, anger, and fear. Within each of these categories are levels of intensity ranging from mild to severe, and it's important for you to become more aware when you are experiencing the milder forms of the emotions so as to prevent their escalation and intensification.

Guilt

Guilt is experienced when we act in a way that is contrary to our and/or society's standards of right or wrong, good or bad. Guilt can emerge from old parental messages that help set our criteria for personal expectations for our behavior and attitudes. While shame can also result from these sources, guilt differs in that we feel that we behaved in a way that does not meet our standards, even when these standards are culturally or family determined. Guilt, unlike shame, is subject to atonement. That is, you can perform acts to make up for the offense that produced your guilt.

For example, you may feel guilty because you forgot a friend's birthday. You can atone for your lapse by giving them a belated birthday card, taking them to lunch, or giving them a gift. A work-related example could be when your mistake in a report is pointed out and you correct it. Or when you do not follow directions and the outcome causes a roadblock for someone else, you could go back and do it correctly, apologize, or resolve to follow directions in the future.

Induced Guilt

Most everyone has felt guilty about something, and most of us try to atone in some way. What is frustrating in relationships with destructive narcissists is the ease with which they are able to induce guilt in others and the futility of trying to atone. They seem able to consistently deepen others' guilt feelings into the more difficult shame-based feelings. Preventing guilt from becoming shame is important because of the distinction between guilt and shame. We can atone for guilt, but shame occurs around feelings that we are fatally flawed. Shame-based feelings suggest that nothing can atone for these flaws and there is nothing we can do to overcome them. In contrast, there is the possibility that we can forgive ourselves and that others can forgive us when we think or do something that produces guilt.

When you work with or for destructive narcissists, you will probably experience considerable guilt. They seem particularly good at ferreting out errors made by others and off-loading their mistakes on others. You will come in for your share of blame and criticism for both mistakes you make and for those made by destructive narcissists. Remember, these people do not ever consider themselves at fault or to blame for anything. Even when they appear to assume responsibility, they often find ways to indicate or accuse others of negligence that caused them to make the mistake.

Contributors to Guilt

Some of your guilt can arise because of choices you make. For example, you may be rushed and choose not to proof a report one more time because you already proofed it twice. However, when you finally turn in the report it turns out that it contains some incorrect figures. When the errors are found and the destructive narcissist comes down on you, you then feel guilty for not having been more careful and triple-checking the report before it was submitted.

A major contribution to guilty feelings when working with or for destructive narcissists is your tendency to react to their criticisms and accusations of blame as you did with your parents when you were a child or adolescent. Reflect on your reactions after an interaction with a destructive narcissist where you felt guilty, and you will probably be able to see the similarities in your reactions to them and how you used to react to your parents.

Everyone has some old parental messages that produce feelings of guilt. Old parental messages can be about almost anything such as:

- being thoughtful and kind,

- following directions,

- paying attention to details,

- checking your work carefully,

- not letting others take advantage of you,

- looking out for or taking care of those less fortunate than you,

- abiding by your religious principles,

- attending church, and so on.

Almost everyone has hundreds of parental messages that guide personal notions of good and bad, right and wrong. These were internalized and continue to play a major role in shaping your behavior and attitudes as an adult.

Although guilt carries the possibility of atonement, you will find it almost impossible to ever atone for anything when dealing with destructive narcissists. They will never forget a mistake and will take every opportunity to remind you and everyone else of your errors. Nothing you say or do will prevent them from assuming a superior attitude and letting you know that they are better than you are because you made a mistake.

Susceptibility to Emotional Contagion

Your susceptibility to emotional contagion also plays a role in the ease with which your guilt feelings are triggered. This concept was described in the chapter on projections and projective identifications. You may be "catching" some feelings from the destructive narcissist, identifying with the feelings they're sending your way then acting on the identification, and this can easily produce feelings of guilt.

An example can illustrate this kind of emotional contagion. Let's stick with the incident of not triple-checking figures in a report before it was submitted. The error is brought to your attention by the destructive narcissist. Generally, when you make a mistake you have a momentary flash of guilt, but most of your energy goes into correcting the mistake. You probably accept the blame and apologize, resolving to not make this mistake again.

However, in this interaction with the destructive narcissist, your acceptance of blame does not appear to satisfy them and they go on to point out other mistakes you've made and how unsatisfactory you are. You may then start to have more intense guilt feelings. This isn't necessarily because you accept or realize that you are making numerous mistakes, as you probably are not making more mistakes than anyone else. Your guilt feelings may intensify in part because of projections from the destructive narcissist that you incorporate, identify with, and are now acting on. You may be experiencing both your personal guilt *and* the guilt you "caught" from the destructive narcissist as part of a projective identification. That is, part of your feelings are those that stem from your values and concepts about right and wrong and about what is good and bad, and part of what you are experiencing may be coming from the other person. The projective identification piece is also more difficult to get rid of, and this can be one reason why feelings like guilt, shame, anger, and fear linger when usually you are able to let go of unpleasant feelings. These linger because they did not originate with you. For our purposes, it is enough at this point simply to have some reasonable explanation for what you're experiencing. These may not be the only reasons or explanations but they can form a working assumption that will allow you to get some perspective on the experience.

Shame

Shame is more difficult to deal with, as it goes to the very core of our being. Shame results when we are faced with knowing or believing that our essential being or essential self is flawed. We are not whole, perfect, or without fault and are fated or doomed to remain that way. Deep within us we believe that there is no hope that we can ever be better. Thus, we seek to hide our "shameful self" from others so that they will not despise us for our flaws. We despise our flaws and feel that others will also see and despise them. A lot of time and energy goes into hiding and repressing our shame.

Shame, like guilt, develops out of parental messages and cultural expectations of just how we are expected to be, as contrasted with how we are to act and think, which are the basis for guilt. Shame is on a deeper level, one that speaks to our perception of our personal self that develops from birth. Thus, many of the antecedents for shame may be lost to our conscious awareness because they may have occurred during infancy and early childhood. The antecedents are not as important here as is your understanding of how your shame may have developed.

Levels of Shame

Shame-based feelings can also range from mild to severe. Milder feelings, such as embarrassment, are common to almost everyone. There are few people who have never experienced feelings of humiliation at some time. Indeed, if you work with or for a destructive narcissist you are unlikely to escape without experiencing embarrassment or humiliation. Destructive narcissists may even seem at times to deliberately try to say and do things that are disparaging, demeaning, and devaluing, any of which can produce humiliation or shame in the target of their remarks or acts.

An example of a shame-producing remark could be as follows. Suppose you were given a task to do that was dependent on previous tasks being completed in a timely way by others, one of which is a coworker who is a destructive narcissist. This person does submit their product to you on time, but it is incorrect and incomplete so that you cannot do your task. You try to talk with the coworker and get them to redo the task, but during the conversation they begin to blame you and say that you don't know what you're talking about and that you are wrong. At this point you are confident that you are correct and begin to try and be specific about the errors. You point out that you cannot do your task until they do their part correctly. Nothing you say makes any difference to them and he or she makes comments about you that attack your competence. If you have ever previously made a mistake and the destructive narcissist knows it, they will bring it into the conversation. They may even attack your personality or physical looks. You will probably make the mistake of trying to respond to the comments or attacks. If you stay focused on the task and refuse to respond, or ask that the conversation stay focused, this person will charge you with something like trying to make them look bad for your own benefit. You may even find that they make these disparaging comments about you to your coworkers and your boss. You do not have the means or opportunity to respond since you are unlikely to be present when such remarks are made. This situation produces frustration along with feelings of shame about not being perfect or even good enough, as the remarks the destructive narcissist makes are calculated to point out your flaws.

Personal Shame

There are many other examples that I could offer, but it's not necessarily worthwhile because what is considered to be shameful varies from person to person. Comments that are embarrassing or humiliating to one person may not be so to someone else. For example, to some women it can be humiliating to be called a "bitch," whereas to other women being called a bitch only produces the reaction of, "What's your point?" The important thing to remember is that some of your reactions to the destructive narcissist can arise from your personal, deep-seated perception of how your essential self is flawed. Another frustrating thing about shame is that you cannot atone for shame as you can for guilt.

A Guilty Overlay

It is possible to have an overlay of guilt on your shame—that is, you experience both guilt and shame. Let's revisit the previous example to illustrate how this can work. When guilt is an overlay of the shame experienced for making mistakes and not being perfect, you could atone for the mistakes by:

- openly acknowledging that you did make the mistake,

- taking action to correct the mistake, and

- instituting procedures or resolving to guard against this kind of mistake in the future.

Unfortunately, the shame would still exist, as you would internally use the mistake as evidence of your flaws. A considerable amount of shame can remain on an unconscious level and continue to be the basis for negative feelings without our being consciously aware that what we experience is shame-based. Guilt is much easier to deal with than is shame, although both are difficult.

Hiding and Masking Shame

Hiding or masking your shame is a common reaction. Shame is very painful, and we fear that others will reject us if they could see our "shameful" selves. For example, some of what appears to be anger and aggression are masked shame. Becoming angry or aggressive prevents others from perceiving that we are shamed. Another way to mask shame is by distracting others from your shame by focusing on something else. Other ways of masking and hiding shame is through the use of defenses where you can both protect yourself from feeling shamed and keep others unaware of your shame. Some of what you experience in interactions with the destructive narcissist is masked and hidden shame.

Understanding Our Shame

The primary task is to understand when we are shamed. Shame is not only experienced as embarrassment or humiliation but also can be seen in feeling discouraged or disappointed in yourself that you did not measure up to expectations (usually expectations that others have of you), or in feeling that you are inadequate or incompetent. Becoming frustrated with yourself may also be masked shame. The underlying assumption is that you should be perfect and that failure means that you are essentially flawed.

Another important point that may be of help is that experienced therapists can also experience shame when confronted with the pathological narcissist, as described by Kernberg (1990) and Masterson (1993). These experienced therapists have done considerable self-exploration and reflection and have worked through much of their unfinished business from the past. In addition, they usually have numerous years of experience as therapists successfully working with a variety of problems and conditions, but even with this extensive experience are unable to keep themselves from experiencing shame with the pathological narcissist. If these professionals also have this problem, then it is no wonder that those who are not mental-health professionals are subject to the same feelings after interacting with someone who has a destructive narcissistic pattern.

Anger

Anger is a response to a perceived threat. It is a protective device to guard against being hurt or destroyed that has both physical and psychological implications. Anger also appears to exhibit itself in levels of intensity ranging from mild to explosive, although the highest level of intensity can still be under the individual's control.

Many people fear their own anger because they are not sure they can control it. They fear others' anger because of past experiences where people in their world became angry and this resulted in harm. But part of the fear may come from their apprehension over personal control of their own anger; that is, they fear that they will become out of control and that the consequences of losing control will be devastating for themselves and for others.

One common reaction to interactions with the destructive narcissist is anger, followed closely by rage and fury. We seem to skip the milder forms of anger such as irritation and annoyance and go right to the more intense forms. This seems to be what happens all too often when interacting with a destructive narcissist.

The other troubling aspect of anger is that once we become angry, the feeling lingers for a long time, and we may even find ourselves displacing that anger on those we hold nearest and dearest. This, of course, does nothing to foster meaningful and satisfying relationships.

Do Not Try to Eliminate Your Anger

The task is not to eliminate anger. It is more constructive to accept and understand that you are perceiving something or someone as a threat and that your anger is the primitive reaction that prepares you to protect against the threat. On the other hand, anger and rage in the workplace is also harmful, as it works against you and is also a threat to your well-being and productivity. This is the primary reason why you need to understand your anger and to use coping strategies to control it rather than expressing it in ways that may be counterproductive to your health and welfare.

Numerous articles and books are available on managing anger, some of which tie management to your type of anger and personality. There are also aids available to help you cope with anger in others. This presentation will not try to duplicate those aids but will attempt to present information that may help you understand your own anger and how to keep it from negatively impacting your image and productivity at work.

Destructive narcissists can trigger your anger, sometimes very easily. The longer you work with that person and the more interactions you have, the easier it is for them to get under your skin. It could be said that you allow yourself to become angry, and there is some validity to that perspective. But it could also be that some of the anger you experience is a result of the projections and projective identifications from the destructive narcissist. Just as they may be projecting guilt your way, so can they project anger. In this case, one reason that you are unable to easily let go of your anger is that all of it did not originate from your perception of a threat.

Anger-Management Techniques

When I teach or present anger-management techniques, the emphasis is on becoming aware of milder forms of anger such as irritation or annoyance. Irritations are fleeting and can be easily dissipated. However, if they linger and build over time, or we allow an event or action to occur that violates some cherished attitude or value, annoyance can result. We find it relatively easy to ignore, let go of, or do something about things that annoy us. This is why, in anger management, the emphasis is on becoming aware of irritations and/or annoyances and taking steps to resolve them before they build.

This approach, however, will not work when dealing with destructive narcissists. They are able to say and do things that are much more threatening to the essential self, resulting in almost instantaneous anger or rage. Even when you resolve that you will not become angry, often you find that your resolve was to no avail, and you do become angry. There may be times when you are tightly controlled and are able to interact with the destructive narcissist without displaying your anger or even being consciously aware that you're angry until you are away from the person. After the interaction is over, you realize that you are very angry. Your body is tense, teeth clenched and jaw tight, hands balled into fists, and stomach upset or churning. Some even feel hot in their chest or head. Tuning into irritation or annoyance is somewhat futile under these circumstances.

The most effective strategies for managing your anger under these circumstances are to:

- withdraw,

- use thought-stopping techniques, and/or

- employ your emotional insulation.

These are explained in more detail in the section on coping strategies later in this chapter.

Costs of Sustained Anger

The costs of sustained anger over a period of time can be high. Physical health, emotional health, and quality of relationships can all suffer and degrade the quality of life. While you are paying the costs of your anger, the destructive narcissist is unaffected. Others' anger has little or no effect on them, except when the person who is angry is perceived by destructive narcissists to be of greater status or to be someone who has something they want or need. You walk around churned up, and they are perfectly okay. You may find it impossible to avoid becoming angry when dealing with the destructive narcissist and may have to accept that reasonable goals are to better manage your anger and to learn how to dissipate it so that it does not negatively impact your physical and emotional health or your relationships. It's possible to accomplish all of these goals, but it will take some self-understanding, acceptance of personal limitations, and hard work. Learning to manage and dissipate anger is a process, and it does not happen all at once.

Fear

Fear is the final category of emotions discussed in this chapter. Fear also occurs in response to a perceived threat and is a defense against being destroyed or engulfed. Fear acts as one way the individual can understand that there is a threat and take steps to save him- or herself.

Fear differs from anger as a response in that anger is the response to anticipation of harm or pain, whereas fear anticipates extinction. Destructive narcissists can be a powerful threat to our well-being as well as our essential selves, which is why our anger and fear are so easily triggered. There also are other reasons related to past experiences and unfinished business that are not discussed here.

It can be difficult to recognize and accept that fear is being experienced as a response to someone. Our objective logical self is able to reason that there is no overt evidence of a threat. However, our more primitive self perceives something about the destructive narcissist that signals danger, and the body responds with anger or fear.

Gradations of Fear

Fear is also experienced as apprehension, dread, or terror. Apprehension and dread are milder forms, and terror is the most extreme. When fear is also defined as apprehension or dread, you may find that you have indeed experienced fear in interactions with destructive narcissists. After several unpleasant experiences you may dread having to interact with them and manufacture reasons to avoid having to do so. You may also find that you are apprehensive about the possibility that you will have to talk or listen to them, another indication that fear is being experienced.

These are all uncomfortable feelings, even though the fear may not escalate to terror. Becoming aware and accepting that you perceive the other person as a threat to your sense of safety on some level are essential steps in understanding and managing your fear.

You may be reacting to your unacknowledged fear on an unconscious level. For example, you see the destructive narcissist coming down the hall and you veer off to the bathroom or remember something you left at your desk and turn around to go back. Another example could be changing your usual route to avoid any possibility of having to talk to them. You can never predict whether the destructive narcissist will be pleasant and charming or if he or she will lash out and be blaming, disparaging, and demeaning of you.

Guilt, shame, and anger also are involved, but fear of being engulfed or destroyed underlies much of our emotional reaction to a destructive narcissist.

Coping Strategies

The best and most enduring coping strategy involves learning to understand yourself and the antecedents of your responses. For example, understand why your response was shame-based and what parental or cultural messages and dictates underlie your responses. Identifying and understanding these help you to be more aware of when you are having a response based on your personal issues, which, in turn, can allow you to choose if you want to continue the response (continue to listen to and abide by an old parental message). This strategy takes considerable time and effort and it would be helpful to have guidance from a mental-health professional. This is a long-term approach.

There are also some shorter-term strategies and techniques that can be helpful. These are intended to provide you with some degree of protection and give you an opportunity to reflect on what is causing the reaction. It may be difficult to accept that you do not have to let what destructive narcissists say or do or a particular attitude of theirs arouse unpleasant feelings. You may even believe that you are somewhat helpless to prevent yourself from experiencing these emotions. Both assumptions may be true; you do not have to respond as you do, but you are also somewhat helpless to prevent your response. You are in the position of both having control and not having control. This paradox contributes to much of the inability to disperse your unpleasant feelings.

Wanting to Change the Self-Absorbed Person

Another important point is that you are probably continuing to hope for change or are working to change the destructive narcissist. If you do hope or have a notion that you can effect change, you are indulging in a fantasy. It is also difficult to accept that you or almost anyone else can have no effect on the destructive narcissist. It's not that they see their destructive or underdeveloped narcissism and do nothing about it—they cannot see it, just as you do not see your own areas of underdeveloped narcissism. This is a blind spot for everyone, and until the person is willing to risk the kind of self-exploration needed to develop healthy adult narcissism, change will not occur. This is not to say that change in behavior cannot be forced—it can. However, the kind of change that is enduring and internalized is not usually amenable to force.

Giving up the fantasy of effecting change in the other person is a very important step in managing your emotions. It is much more constructive and effective to work to change your behavior and attitudes than it is to continue to hope for change in another person. You have to realize and accept that you can never be powerful enough, empathic enough, or perfect enough to effect what you want to change in the other person. The only change over which you have any control is over your own behaviors, attitudes, and feelings.

Short-Term Strategies

There are some short-term strategies and techniques that you can use to protect yourself and cope with the more distressing feelings aroused by the behaviors of the destructive narcissist. These are easily implemented but do require conscious and constant attention. Effective strategies are:

- emotional insulation,
- cognitive techniques,
- humor, and
- creativity.

Emotional Insulation

Insulating and protecting yourself from the destructive narcissist's projections and projective identifications can help you manage your feelings by insuring that what you experience is indeed your "stuff" and not added feelings caught from or induced by the other person. For example, you can remain annoyed instead of becoming angry. You probably can dissipate your annoyance easier than you can your anger.

Techniques for emotionally insulating yourself, such as visualizing a wall between you, are described in a previous chapter. The trick is to constantly use whatever techniques you choose. It takes practice, an awareness of the need to shield yourself, and a determination to be ever alert. Your insulation must be in place before interacting with the destructive narcissist in order for it to be effective.

On the other hand, you do not want to put this barrier between yourself and others with whom you want to establish or maintain a positive relationship. Try to consciously use your emotional insulation only when needed and not allow it to become your standard mode. It can also prevent you from perceiving relevant input needed to be empathic with others, you do not want to lose this ability with "safe" people.

Cognitive Techniques

Some cognitive techniques that may be helpful are:

- thought stopping,

- analyzing instead of only feeling,

- self-affirmations, and

- resolving your cognitive distortions about personal assumptions, such as the need to be perfect.

Thought stopping means consciously distracting yourself from unproductive or potentially depressing self-talk. For example, say you're involved in an interaction with destructive narcissists who are blaming you for their errors and you find that your anger is escalating to rage. In this situation, you can consciously decide to stop the escalation. Try thinking, "Hey, I'm becoming angry, and I don't want to go there. I will think about something else." Think about anything besides the issue at hand or even change the subject. In this situation you have also decided not to focus on blame at that point. You neither attack nor defend—you just stop. What you may find is that by using thought stopping you de-escalate your feelings and this makes them easier for you to manage.

Analyzing is another way of cognitively stepping back and observing what you are doing. Instead of analyzing after the fact, try interrupting your slide into guilt, shame, anger, or fear by observing yourself and thinking about why you're responding in that way. Using the previous example of becoming angry at being unfairly blamed, you could analyze your response by first noting that you are becoming angry and asking yourself what about the situation is threatening to you. This is also a "Why is this making me angry?" question, although a better way of framing the question would be, "Why am I allowing myself to become angry?"

The perceived threat may be real or imaginary, but you are reacting as if it were real. Analyzing can also help you to understand the validity of your perception, and the process of analysis also halts escalation of the emotion's intensity.

Self-affirmations are reminders to yourself that you have strengths, that whatever your errors, inadequacies, or lapses, you also have abilities, competencies, and aptitudes and that these outweigh or offset these mistakes. Self-affirmations also arrest the slide into more intense unpleasant emotions. You emphasize your positive points rather than any negative ones.

Develop a set of personal self-affirmations by making a list of your accomplishments, talents, and strengths. Write some of these on a card and carry the card with you. Make a point of reading your card every day. When interacting with a destructive narcissist and reacting with guilt or shame, mentally say a few of your self-affirmations. Try not to have self-affirmations that say you will not do or feel something, as these do not work as well as reminders of your strengths. For example, it probably will not be effective for you to affirm that you will not let the person make you guilty, shamed, angry, or fearful, or that you will not feel a certain way. It is more effective to affirm that you have positive characteristics and accomplishments.

Cognitive distortions are self-statements that are unrealistic or unreasonable. For example, it is both unrealistic and unreasonable to expect that you will never make a mistake. Most everyone would agree with that statement on the surface. The distortion part comes into play when individuals also have a deep-seated belief that they shouldn't ever make mistakes and attribute any error to an essential, damning flaw. When you buy into a distortion, you not only accept the blame, you embrace and embellish it.

Become aware of your cognitive distortions. When you experience guilt or shame, reflect on what these feelings may be telling you about your distorted self-statements. Remind yourself that you do not have to continue to buy into these distortions or berate yourself.

Examples of some common cognitive distortions are:

- I must do everything perfectly.
- Everyone must like me.
- It is essential that I be accepted by everyone.
- I must never make a mistake.
- I should never get frustrated.
- Others should do what I want them to do.
- If others do not agree with me then I must be wrong.
- It is up to me to make sure things run smoothly.

Humor

Kohut (1976) proposed that one characteristic of healthy adult narcissism is humor. The ability to see the funny side of a situation is a very valuable technique for managing your unpleasant feelings resulting from interactions with a destructive narcissist. This is not to say that you laugh at these people. Laughing at someone is a demeaning, devaluing act and is not advised. Seeing humor in the situation or in yourself is what can be helpful.

You can defuse the intensity of unpleasant feelings by using humor, when appropriate. What can be of the most use is not an open display of humor, but your own internal, private awareness of the humorous aspects of the situation. You can also use humor to distract yourself from the negative situation by thinking of something funny. You do not have to share what was funny, you can keep it to yourself.

For example, you could laugh to yourself at the absurdity of what the destructive narcissist is saying instead of becoming angry. Pointing out the absurdity would be counterproductive as he or she would not accept what you are saying, thus infuriating you even further. It's enough for you to realize that what they are saying is absurd and to see the humor. It helps dissipate the unpleasant feeling.

Laughter is a wonderful tension and stress reducer. If you must constantly interact with a destructive narcissist, find some way to laugh each day. And I don't mean just a chuckle—give it a real laugh.

There are numerous ways to get some humor in everyday life. A couple of friends and I had a lot of fun and laughter from developing a list of "What the hells . . ." We came up with quite a few, like what the hell are you doing, thinking of, is that, etc. As long as your humor does not demean or devalue others, take delight in someone's misfortune, or hurt someone, the humor is appropriate and can help dissipate unpleasant feelings. A sense of well-being can result from a hearty laugh.

Creativity

Expand your creative endeavors. Creativity is also a characteristic of healthy adult narcissism and can take many forms. Creativity is not limited to the fine and performing arts but can be an individual expression in almost everything. Find and/or recover your creativity.

Hobbies, work-related activities, and other life activities are all sources for creative endeavors. If you already have a talent, do something to increase your expertise or learn another process. If you have a hobby, become more involved in it and share it with someone. For example, if you do woodworking as a hobby, consider teaching it to children or senior citizens. There are many opportunities to do things like this in almost every community. Outlets for increasing your creativity are vast and very rewarding.

If you are not aware of a personal talent, you could try something that appeals to you. For example, take a cooking class or a cake-decorating class, try calligraphy, begin a collection of something, etc. Once you begin some activity, you will begin to think of how to expand, enhance, and explore it, and that leads to creativity.

At the very least you will be distracted from the unpleasant feelings experienced in interactions with the destructive narcissist.

Summary

There are steps you can take to minimize the impact of unpleasant feelings that come up when constantly interacting with destructive narcissists. You may not be able to eliminate these feelings, but you can reduce their impact and manage them. Essential to better managing these feelings is giving up any notion or hope you may have that you can change destructive narcissists. You can only work on yourself.

You do not have to just suffer and "take it" when working with or for a destructive narcissist—you can work to help yourself. You now know what that person is doing that is troubling to you and how you may be contributing to your own distress and you have a list of suggested strategies for making your personal work environment better. You can make small changes in your behavior and attitudes that will be immensely helpful. Good luck in all your endeavors.

References

American Psychiatric Association. 1994. *Diagnostic and Statistical Manual of Mental Disorders*, 4th ed. Washington, D.C.: American Psychiatric Association.

Berube, M. 1999. *Webster's II New College Dictionary*. Boston: Houghton Mifflin.

Brown, N. 1998. *The Destructive Narcissistic Pattern*. Westport, CT: Praeger.

Hafen, B., K. Karren, K. Frandsen, and N. L. Smith. 1996. *Mind/Body Health*. Boston: Allyn and Bacon.

Johnson, D., and F. Johnson. 1996. *Joining Together*. 6th ed. Boston: Allyn and Bacon

Kernberg, O. 1990. *Borderline Conditions and Pathological Narcissism*. Northvale, NJ: Jason Aronson Inc.

Kohut, H. 1977. *The Restoration of the Self*. New York: International Universities Press.

Masterson, J. F. 1993. *The Emerging Self: A Developmental, Self and Object Relations Approach to the Treatment of the Closet Narcissistic Disorder of the Self*. New York: Brunner/Mazel.

Pease, A. 1984. *Signals*. New York: Bantam Books

Yalom, I. 1995. *The Theory and Practice of Group Psychotherapy*. New York: Basic Books

Some Other
New Harbinger Titles

Printed in the United States
106105LV00001B/197/A

9 781572 242920